2010 SUPPLEMENT TO
CASES AND MATERIALS ON
LEGISLATION

STATUTES AND THE CREATION
OF PUBLIC POLICY
Fourth Edition

■ ■ ■

By
William N. Eskridge, Jr.
John A. Garver Professor of Jurisprudence
Yale University

Philip P. Frickey
Late Alexander F. & May T. Morrison Professor of Law
University of California, Berkeley

Elizabeth Garrett
France R. and John J. Duggan Professor of Law
Political Science and Public Policy
University of Southern California

AMERICAN CASEBOOK SERIES®

WEST.
A Thomson Reuters business

Mat #41009836

American Casebook Series is a trademark registered in the U.S. Patent and Trademark Office.

© 2010 Thomson Reuters
    610 Opperman Drive
    St. Paul, MN 55123
    1–800–313–9378

Printed in the United States of America

ISBN: 978–0–314–92633–3

PREFACE

This supplement incorporates important developments that have arisen since the publication of the fourth edition of our casebook in 2007. We welcome suggestions and comments as we begin planning the fifth edition of the book.

We thank Yale and USC Gould law schools for generous summer support. Alexander Fullman (USC), Ian Magladry (USC), Brian Richardson (Yale), and Matthew Shapiro (Yale) provided valuable research assistance. We are grateful for the suggestions that Professors Craig Oren and Peter Strauss have provided with respect to the fourth edition; some are reflected here, and others will be incorporated into the next edition. We also appreciate Susan Wampler's excellent copy-editing skills and help throughout this process.

Our friend, colleague, and co-author Philip P. Frickey passed away as we were about to go to press. It is with immense sadness for our personal loss, and the loss of one of the great thinkers and scholars in this field, that we dedicate this publication to his memory.

WILLIAM N. ESKRIDGE, JR.

ELIZABETH GARRETT

July 2010

TABLE OF CONTENTS

Table of Cases

The principal cases are in bold type. Cases cited or discussed in the text are in roman type. References are to pages. Cases cited in principal cases and within other quoted materials are not included.

2010 SUPPLEMENT TO
CASES AND MATERIALS ON
LEGISLATION
STATUTES AND THE CREATION
OF PUBLIC POLICY
Fourth Edition

CHAPTER 1

AN INTRODUCTION TO LEGISLATION

■ ■ ■

SECTION 1. THE STORY OF THE CIVIL RIGHTS ACT OF 1964 AND THE PROCEDURES OF STATUTE–CREATION

Page 29. Delete the first full sentence and replace with the following:

The House, now controlled by Democrats, did not include the term limitation on committee chairs when it adopted the new rules for the 111th Congress in 2009.

Page 35. Delete the second full sentence and replace with the following:

One-fifth of a quorum may demand a roll-call vote in either chamber; when the House is sitting as a Committee of the Whole, the Chair must order a recorded vote if 25 members request it.

Page 36. Add the following at the end of the discussion of unorthodox legislation:

The use of unorthodox lawmaking procedures has continued and increased in the first Congresses of the 2000s. For example, an average of one in five major legislative proposals bypassed House committees in the first Congresses of this century and, in the 107th Congress, 41% of major legislation went to the Senate floor without first going to a committee. Barbara Sinclair, *Unorthodox Lawmaking: New Legislative Processes in the U.S. Congress* 17, 47 (3d ed. 2007). It remains the case that major legislation, which is more likely to be considered through processes that do not mirror the textbook description, is more likely to be enacted. During the 100th through the 106th Congresses, 14% of bills introduced in the House were passed by that chamber, and 24% of Senate proposals emerged from the Senate. For major legislation, 88% of House proposals passed that body, and 72% of Senate bills made it through. Moreover, it continues to be the case that about 60% of major legislation is enacted into law. Sinclair, *supra*, at 271–72.

SECTION 3. TITLE VII: INTERPRETIVE ISSUES AND POLITICAL THEORIES

C. *GRIGGS* REVISITED: COURT VERSUS CONGRESS

2. The Civil Rights Act of 1991

Page 120. Add the following Case and Note right before *A Transitional Note*:

Ricci v. DeStefano, 129 S.Ct. 2658 (2009). In 2003, 118 New Haven firefighters took examinations to qualify for promotion to the rank of lieutenant or captain. Promotion examinations were infrequent, so the stakes were high. The results would determine which firefighters would be considered for promotions during the next two years, and the order in which they would be considered. The City contracted with Industrial/Organizational Solutions, Inc. (IOS), a well-regarded job-testing firm for police and fire departments, to develop and administer the examinations. IOS representatives worked with officials and firefighters (including minority firefighters) within the department to develop written and oral tests that would be related to the job requirements and fair to all groups.

Seventy-seven candidates completed the lieutenant examination—43 persons of European ancestry, 19 African ancestry, and 15 Latino ancestry. Of those, 34 candidates passed—25 European Americans, 6 African Americans, and 3 Latino Americans. Eight lieutenant positions were vacant at the time of the examination; the top 10 candidates were eligible for an immediate promotion to lieutenant, and all were of European ancestry. Subsequent vacancies would have allowed at least three African-American candidates to be considered for promotion to lieutenant.

Forty-one candidates completed the captain examination—25 European Americans, 8 African Americans, and 8 Latino Americans. Of those, 22 candidates passed—16 European Americans, 3 African Americans, and 3 Latino Americans. Seven captain positions were vacant at the time of the examination; 9 candidates were eligible for an immediate promotion to captain—7 European Americans and 2 Latino Americans.

When the examination results showed that European–American candidates had outperformed minority candidates, Mayor John DeStefano and other local politicians opened a public debate that turned rancorous. Some firefighters argued the tests should be discarded because the results showed the tests to be discriminatory. They threatened a discrimination lawsuit if the City made promotions based on the tests. Other firefighters said the exams were neutral, and they threatened a discrimination lawsuit if the City, relying on the statistical racial disparity, ignored the test results and denied promotions to the candidates who had performed well. In the end the City took the side of those who protested the test results. The Mayor threw out the examinations.

Certain white and Latino firefighters, who likely would have been promoted based on their good test performance, sued the City and some of its officials. They alleged that, by discarding the test results, the City and the named officials discriminated against the plaintiffs based on their race, in violation of Title VII and the Equal Protection Clause. The City defended its actions, arguing that, if officials had certified the results, they could have faced liability under Title VII for adopting a practice that had a disparate impact on the minority firefighters.

The District Court granted summary judgment for the City, and the Court of Appeals (in a panel that included Judge, now Justice, Sonia Sotomayor) affirmed. Joined by Chief Justice Roberts and Justices Scalia, Thomas, and Alito, **Justice Kennedy**'s opinion for the Court ruled that "race-based action like the City's in this case is impermissible under Title VII unless the employer can demonstrate a strong basis in evidence that, had it not taken the action, it would have been liable under the disparate-impact statute. The respondents, we further determine, cannot meet that threshold standard. As a result, the City's action in discarding the tests was a violation of Title VII." Because New Haven's action violated Title VII, the Court did not reach the constitutional (equal protection) challenge.

Justice Kennedy's opinion rejected the firefighters' arguments that New Haven's disparate treatment of them (because of their white race) could not be justified by the threat of disparate impact lawsuits if the City had followed the test results. Reading the 1964 and 1991 Acts together, the Court held that an employer may adopt voluntary race-based remedies for apparent violations of the disparate impact provision of the 1991 Act, without violating the disparate treatment provision of the 1964 Act. The opinion also rejected the City's argument that a "good faith" belief that the tests violated the disparate impact provision would justify race-based remedies; such a lenient standard would, Justice Kennedy feared, open the door to a "de facto quota system," inconsistent with the premises of Title VII. Cf. § 703(j).

"In searching for a standard that strikes a more appropriate balance, we note that this Court has considered cases similar to this one, albeit in the context of the Equal Protection Clause of the Fourteenth Amendment. The Court has held that certain government actions to remedy past racial discrimination—actions that are themselves based on race—are constitutional only where there is a 'strong basis in evidence' that the remedial actions were necessary." *Richmond v. J.A. Croson Co.*, 488 U.S. 469, 500 (1989) (O'Connor, J., for a majority), quoting *Wygant v. Jackson Bd. of Educ.*, 476 U.S. 267, 277 (1986) (Powell, J., for a plurality).

"The standard leaves ample room for employers' voluntary compliance efforts, which are essential to the statutory scheme and to Congress's efforts to eradicate workplace discrimination. And the standard appropriately constrains employers' discretion in making race-based decisions: It limits that discretion to cases in which there is a strong basis in evidence of disparate-impact liability, but it is not so restrictive that it allows employers to act only when there is a provable, actual violation." At no point did Justice Kennedy cite *Weber* (casebook, pp. 88–100), and his opinion paid only glancing reference to *Johnson* (casebook, pp. 104–14).

Was there a "strong basis in evidence" for the City to conclude that it would face disparate impact liability if it followed the test results? The disparate racial impact of the tests made out a prima facie case for liability under the 1991 Act, but Justice Kennedy ruled that the City had no "strong basis" to believe that its business necessity defense would not prevail in potential lawsuits.

Writing also for Justices Stevens, Souter, and Breyer, **Justice Ginsburg** dissented. She started with a broader context, namely, the long history of exclusion for African- and Latino-American citizens from municipal police and firefighting jobs, including near-total exclusion for most of New Haven's history. In light of this history of exclusion, especially in the officer ranks, New Haven had a great deal of discretion to question the results of a test that statistically favored persons of European descent. At public meetings (before the test results had been released), several observers claimed that the test had several questions not relevant to firefighting duties or command; others pointed out that some firefighters had earlier access to study materials than others did; one participant pointed out that a neighboring city had a racially imbalanced force until it abandoned the use of standardized tests such as this one. Experts told the City that a more problem-oriented approach would have been practical and would probably have had a less racially discriminatory impact.

"Congress [has] declared unambiguously that selection criteria operating to the disadvantage of minority group members can be retained only if justified by business necessity. In keeping with Congress' design, employers who reject such criteria due to reasonable doubts about their reliability can hardly be held to have engaged in discrimination 'because of' race. A reasonable endeavor to comply with the law and to ensure that qualified candidates of all races have a fair opportunity to compete is simply not what Congress meant to interdict. I would therefore hold that an employer who jettisons a selection device when its disproportionate racial impact becomes apparent does not violate Title VII's disparate-treatment bar automatically or at all, subject to this key condition: The employer must have good cause to believe the device would not withstand examination for business necessity."

Justice Ginsburg maintained that her approach was more consistent with the EEOC's longstanding guidance on remedial race-based affirmative action permissible under Title VII and with the Court's precedents, specifically *Johnson*. She also argued that equal protection precedents were of "limited utility" because the Equal Protection Clause does **not** regulate state rules that only have a disparate race-based impact; there is no equal protection parallel to *Griggs* (casebook, pp. 42–47) and the 1991 Act's provision for disparate impact liability. Even under the Court's announced standard, Justice Ginsburg maintained that the City had a "strong basis in evidence" to question whether the IOS-developed test really met the business necessity requirement of the 1991 Act. So many questions were raised about the test, and the City had followed it simply because the union insisted on such a test.

Writing also for Justices Scalia and Thomas, **Justice Alito** wrote a concurring opinion that responded to Justice Ginsburg's factual points. Justice Alito's understanding was that the City's volte-face was politically motivated. "Taking into account all the evidence in the summary judgment record, a reasonable jury could find the following. Almost as soon as the City disclosed the racial makeup of the list of firefighters who scored the highest on the exam, the City administration was lobbied by an influential community leader to scrap the test results, and the City administration decided on that course of action before making any real assessment of the possibility of a disparate-impact violation. To achieve that end, the City administration concealed its internal decision but worked—as things turned out, successfully—to persuade the [review board] that acceptance of the test results would be illegal and would expose the City to disparate-impact liability. But in the event that the [review board] was not persuaded, the Mayor, wielding ultimate decision-making authority, was prepared to overrule the [board] immediately. Taking this view of the evidence, a reasonable jury could easily find that the City's real reason for scrapping the test results was not a concern about violating the disparate-impact provision of Title VII but a simple desire to please a politically important racial constituency."

Justice Ginsburg responded that she would be in favor of a remand to see precisely what various options a "reasonable" jury would have accepted. Moreover, Justice Alito's understanding of the decisionmaking ignored the fact that the reviewing board—an unelected, politically insulated group of experts—made the actual decision, and the Mayor did not. Finally, are all "political considerations" tantamount to race discrimination itself? "The real issue, then, is not whether the mayor and his staff were politically motivated; it is whether their attempt to score political points was legitimate (*i.e.*, nondiscriminatory). Were they seeking to exclude white firefighters from promotion (unlikely, as a fair test would undoubtedly result in the addition of white firefighters to the officer ranks), or did they realize, at least belatedly, that their tests could be toppled in a disparate-impact suit? In the latter case, there is no disparate-treatment violation. Justice Alito, I recognize, would disagree. In his view, an employer's action to avoid Title VII disparate-impact liability qualifies as a presumptively improper race-based employment decision. I reject that construction of Title VII. As I see it, when employers endeavor to avoid exposure to disparate-impact liability, they do not thereby encounter liability for disparate treatment."

Notes on the New Haven Firefighters Case and Statutory Allowance for Workplace Affirmative Action

1. *What Is the Law Now?* Obviously, the current Title VII law is the interpretation rendered by the Court majority in *Ricci*—but what is a "strong basis in evidence" for the existence of a *Griggs* violation? For example, would the *Ricci* Court have followed Justice O'Connor in *Johnson*, where she found that the employer had a "firm basis" for remedying prior discrimination (casebook, pp. 108–10)? Recall that Justice Scalia rejected Justice O'Connor's reading of the record, in part because the District Court had found, as a matter of fact, that there had been "no discrimination" against women in *Johnson*.

How can the "strong basis in evidence" standard be administered? Should the EEOC issue a guidance along these lines? If so, what should it say?

2. *Impact of the 1991 Amendments on the Affirmative Action Issue?* The *Ricci* Court rejected a hard no-race-factors-ever interpretation of Title VII in light of the 1991 Amendments. (In a concurring opinion we omitted, Justice Scalia suggested that this might be unconstitutional in a future case.) Interestingly, there was a provision that some lower court judges thought barred affirmative action, namely, new § 703(m), added by the 1991 Amendments:

> An unlawful employment practice is established whenever the complaining party demonstrates that race, color, religion, sex, or national origin was a motivating factor for any employment practice, even though other factors also motivated the practice.

Why did the Court not consider § 703(m) in its construction of Title VII? Indeed, why did über-textualist Justice Scalia not insist upon following § 703(m), to stick to his absolutist position in *Johnson*? (From his perspective, § 703(m) would have the virtues of codifying his *Johnson* position and avoiding the potential constitutional problems with § 703(a) as construed in *Ricci*.)

A reader of legislative history, Justice Kennedy might have been reluctant to rely on § 703(m), because it was added to the 1991 Amendments to override *Price Waterhouse v. Hopkins* (casebook, p. 117), a recent mixed-motives case. There is no evidence that anyone in Congress thought that § 703(m) affected *Johnson* or *Weber*. But why should Justice Scalia care about this kind of evidence? How about § 116 of the 1991 Amendments: "Nothing in the amendments made by this title shall be construed to affect court-ordered remedies, affirmative action, or conciliation agreements, that are in accordance with the law." Does that help explain Scalia's reticence? Or not?

3. *Continuing the Court/Congress/President Civil Rights Game.* Notice how *Ricci* reflects the dynamic potential of the law-implementation process. Soon after the 1964 Act was adopted, the EEOC and the Court pushed Title VII to the left through liberal construction of the disparate impact claim for relief (casebook, pp. 82–87). Congress rejected proposals to trim back Title VII in the 1972 Amendments, and *Weber–Johnson* confirmed the evolution of Title VII toward a more strongly integrationist stance than Congress had probably assumed in 1964.

But the Rehnquist Court pushed the statute in a more conservative direction—and Congress pushed back with the 1991 Amendments. As *Ricci* dramatically illustrates, the 1989 Supreme Court decisions did not push Title VII back to 1964—nor did the 1991 Amendments push Title VII back to the heyday of liberal interpretation in the 1970s. Instead, Title VII's text represents a pretty detailed compromise between the Brennan vision for workplace diversity and the Rehnquist vision for employer color-blindness.

CHAPTER 2

REPRESENTATIONAL STRUCTURES

■ ■ ■

SECTION 1. ELECTORAL STRUCTURES AND EQUALITY VALUES

B. RACE AND ELECTORAL STRUCTURES

2. The Voting Rights Act and Racial Vote Dilution

Page 149. The sentence quoting language from 42 U.S.C. § 1973c in the middle paragraph should read:

To prevent circumvention of the Act by the adoption of other discriminatory methods, § 5 of the Act required that no change in voting qualifications or procedures may be implemented without the prior determination of either the Attorney General or the United States District Court for the District of Columbia that the change "neither has the purpose nor will have the effect of denying or abridging the right to vote on account of race or color." 42 U.S.C. § 1973c.

Page 149–50. Delete the paragraph that begins on page 149 and concludes on page 150, and replace with the following:

The 1965 Act provided that its preclearance requirement would lapse in five years. In 1970, the Act was renewed for another five years, and in 1975 the Act was renewed for another seven years. In 1982, the Act was renewed again, but this time it was extensively amended to terminate the Act's coverage in 25 years and to allow covered jurisdictions more opportunity to bail out of its coverage. Most recently, in 2006, the Act was extended yet again for another 25 years.[x] The Act was substantially unchanged from the 1982 Act with the exception of an alteration to the standard for what constitutes discriminatory purpose and discriminatory

---

x. Although the 2006 legislation passed by votes of 98–0 in the Senate and 390–33 in the House, there was considerable back-room grumbling from Southern legislators chafing at its continuation of preclearance coverage and from a spectrum of legislators concerning the requirement of bilingual ballots. On the conflictual legislative history behind the seeming consensus, see Nathaniel Persily, *The Promise and Pitfalls of the New Voting Rights Act*, 117 Yale L.J. 174 (2007); James Tucker, *The Politics of Persuasion: Passage of the Voting Rights Reauthorization Act of 2006*, 33 J. Legis. 205 (2007). In addition, see generally, *The Future of the Voting Rights Act* (David Epstein, Richard Pildes, Rodolfo de la Garza, & Sharyn O'Halloran eds., 2006); *Voting Rights Act Reauthorization of 2006: Perspectives on Democracy, Participation, and Power* (Ana Henderson ed., 2006); Luis Fuentes–Rohwer, *Understanding the Paradoxical Case of the Voting Rights Act*, 36 Fla. St. U. L. Rev. 697 (2009); Heather Gerken, *A Third Way for the Voting Rights Act: Section 5 and the Opt–In Approach*, 106 Colum. L. Rev. 708 (2006); Michael Kang, *Race and Democratic Contestation*, 117 Yale L.J. 734 (2008).

effect. Congress effectively overturned *Reno v. Bossier Parish School Board*, 528 U.S. 320 (2000), and made it clear that mere discriminatory purpose, regardless of the effect on minorities, is grounds for a denial of preclearance. Furthermore, by overturning *Georgia v. Ashcroft*, 539 U.S. 461 (2003), the Act now requires the denial of preclearance when the voting laws effectively diminish the ability of minorities to elect their preferred candidates of choice.

The Voting Rights Act has been successful in increasing minority registration, voting, and officeholding in the covered jurisdictions.[y] It has also been controversial because it singles out one region of the country, all but labels it as discriminatory, and requires the local and state governments covered by the Act to obtain federal approval before making even the simplest changes in voting procedures (e.g., moving a polling place).[z] Section 5's coverage formula, which was reenacted without change in 2006, has been criticized as being simultaneously overinclusive and underinclusive. For example, in states that do not have substantial histories of racial discrimination, such as Michigan and New Hampshire, certain jurisdictions are still covered. Jurisdictions in Ohio and Florida, where there have been more recent and well-publicized instances of serious voting rights violations, are not covered. The shortcomings of the coverage formula were acknowledged during the congressional debates on reenactment, but "[w]hat became clear throughout the reauthorization process was that a debate over the coverage formula would turn into a debate about the purpose and utility of section 5 itself. Such a debate likely would have led to the complete unraveling of the bill." Nathaniel Persily, *The Promise and Pitfalls of the New Voting Rights Act*, 117 Yale L.J. 174, 208–09 (2007). Moreover, the political concerns about partisan and regional backlash dissuaded Congress from changing the coverage criteria: Ohio and Florida are large and powerful, and the jurisdictions that would be targeted for coverage were controlled by Republicans who were needed for bipartisan support.

SECTION 2.   ELIGIBILITY TO SERVE IN THE LEGISLATURE

A. CONGRESSIONALLY IMPOSED QUALIFICATIONS

Page 208. Add after *Problem 2–3* the following new problem:

Problem 2–3a. When Barack Obama became President of the United States, he left his Senate seat from Illinois vacant. State law allowed the

---

y. See Davidson & Grofman, *supra* (casebook, p. 136, note t); Pildes, *supra* (casebook, p. 136, note t); and the more recent sources cited above concerning the legislative history of the 2006 extension.

z. The technicalities of § 5 are beyond our scope. For decisions involving the application of § 5 (other than those overturned by the 2006 reauthorization, discussed in the text), see, e.g., *Northwest Austin Municipal Utility District Number One v. Holder*, 129 S.Ct. 2504 (2009) (finding that bailout relief was available to a utility district as a political subdivision and thus declining to rule on the constitutionality of preclearance); *Lopez v. Monterey County*, 525 U.S. 266 (1999) (county covered by the Act must preclear electoral changes mandated by changes in state law, even if the state itself is not a covered jurisdiction); *Presley v. Etowah County Comm'n*, 502 U.S. 491 (1992) (decision to shift power from individual commissioners to commission as a whole not covered by § 5).

governor, Democrat Rod Blagojevich, to appoint the successor to serve until the 2010 election. It soon became apparent through federal wiretaps and other evidence that the Governor, who was already under investigation for corruption, was seeking favors from people he was considering for the position. As this controversy raged, Blagojevich announced that he would appoint Roland Burris, a Democrat who had been elected Illinois's first African-American State Comptroller and Attorney General. Soon there were allegations that Burris had discussed a *quid pro quo* with the venal Blagojevich, and his appointment became controversial. Although Burris received appointment papers from the Governor, the Illinois Secretary of State refused to sign them. When Burris arrived in Washington to take his seat, the Secretary of the Senate rejected his credentials because Senate Rule 2, part of the Senate rules since 1884, requires that an appointment include the signatures of both the Governor and Secretary of State. Senate Majority Leader Harry Reid (D–Nev.) and the senior Senator from Illinois, Dick Durbin (D), declared that Burris should not be seated; Reid cited Article I, § 5 of the Constitution that "each House shall be the Judge of the Elections, Returns, and Qualifications of its own Members." Does *Powell v. McCormack* provide guidance as to the Senate's power in this case to scrutinize this appointment and possibly to refuse to seat Burris? What is the appropriate venue to determine Burris' suitability to serve, or is it sufficient that the sitting Governor appointed him, notwithstanding the circumstances of the appointment?

In the end, Burris went to state court, which ruled that state law did not require the Secretary of State's signature for the appointment to be valid, and the Illinois Secretary of State signed a second document acknowledging the appointment to be legally valid. Accordingly, the Secretary of the Senate accepted his credentials, ending the possibility that the case might reach federal court on that ground. But in another twist to the case, the Seventh Circuit ruled that the Seventeenth Amendment requires a special election to fill a Senate vacancy, with any appointment serving temporarily until the election can be held. This decision raises the possibility that Illinois voters will vote to fill the remaining weeks of Obama's Senate term in a special election held on November 2, 2010—the same time as the regular election for the seat's next full term. See *Judge v. Quinn,* 2010 WL 2652204 (7th Cir. 2010).

B. QUALIFICATIONS IMPOSED BY STATES: TERM LIMITATIONS FOR FEDERAL LEGISLATORS

Page 225. Add the following before 3. *Developments in Congress since* U.S. Term Limits:

In 2008, a year before municipal elections, New York City Mayor Michael Bloomberg argued that the two-term limit imposed through a voter initiative should be changed to allow City officials to serve three terms, thereby enabling him to seek another term. He argued that the economic crisis facing the city and the country required continuity of leadership. It may not have been coincidental that he had just abandoned his effort to pursue the presidency of the United States as an independent candidate. The City Council voted, 29 to 22, to extend term limits for city elected officials (including themselves) to three terms, after a spirited debate that included discussion of whether the council could legitimately change a policy adopted by the voters directly. Not only had the voters imposed the term limits in 1993, but they had also rejected in 1995 a referendum supported by the City Council to enlarge the limit to three terms. Because the change was an amendment to the City Charter, the Council had the power to enact the restriction even though it had been adopted by popular vote. Supporters of longer term limits promised that the New York City Charter Revision Commission would consider the issue in hearings in 2010. Mayor Bloomberg was reelected, but by a much narrower margin than he had enjoyed in the previous reelection battle.

Page 225. Delete the penultimate sentence in note 3 and replace with the following:

The House did not re-adopt term limits for committee chairs in the 111th Congress, which was controlled by the Democrats.

C. BALLOT ACCESS PROVISIONS

Page 233. Replace the last sentence of footnote z with the following:

The Supreme Court upheld the nonpartisan, or "top-two," primary that voters adopted to replace the blanket primary, but it left open the possibility of an as-applied challenge if the ballot design and text do not sufficiently alert voters that the party preference expressed by candidates does not mean that the parties have endorsed those candidates. *Washington State Grange v. Washington State Republican Party*, 552 U.S. 442 (2008). The ballot provides next to a candidate's name a statement of which party she prefers, or that she prefers no party, and a candidate is not limited to naming a qualified party. For example, in 2008, some candidates indicated a preference for the "Salmon Yoga Party," the "No Gas Taxes (R) Party," and similar labels, as well as the more traditional political parties. In June 2010, California adopted a similar top-two primary system through the initiative process.

SECTION 3. STRUCTURES OF CAMPAIGN FINANCE

A. THE CONSTITUTIONAL FRAMEWORK: *BUCKLEY v. VALEO*

Page 250. Add the following at the end of the last full paragraph:

The unprecedented involvement of small donors in Barack Obama's successful campaign for the presidency seemed a sign that a political system with more participation by ordinary citizens, and therefore less influence by well-heeled interests, was within reach. President Obama raised more than $746 million in the 2008 presidential election; $181

million of that came from 24% of his donors who contributed $200 or less.[a]
The campaign's sophisticated use of the Internet was primarily responsible for the widespread grassroots involvement, not only in contributing but also in organizing meetings and volunteering. My.BarackObama.com, known as MyBO, used social networking sites to build a close online relationship with Obama supporters; it encouraged repeated small donations using techniques such as matching the small donation with another new donor or charging small recurring donations monthly to supporters' credit cards. Anthony Corrado, Michael Malbin, Thomas Mann, & Norman Ornstein, *Reform in An Age of Networked Campaigns* 12–14 (2010).

Reform advocates have begun to reformulate campaign finance proposals given the potential of the Internet to broaden the group of people participating in campaigns. For example, some have proposed an overhaul of the presidential public financing system so that small contributions receive more generous matching funds (such as a match of three- or four-to-one for contributions of $200 or less) and candidates are not subject to expenditure limits as long as they are spending funds raised from small donations. Given the irrelevance of the current presidential campaign financing system (Obama opted out of the system for both the primary and general elections, as did Hillary Clinton and John McCain for the primaries) and the new model of fundraising that Obama created and maintains, it seems time for substantial change.

Some commentators have counseled that the claims of a new era of the small donor are overstated. Although small donors played an important role in Obama's success, he still received most of his sizable campaign war chest from wealthy individuals. The Campaign Finance Institute revealed that Obama received 80% more money from people giving at least $1,000 than from small donors, and most of the sizable contributions came from 85,000 people, a majority of whom were bundling money for the campaign (see casebook, pp. 253–54, for a discussion of bundling).[b] Although the Obama campaign refused to take money, bundled or otherwise, from registered lobbyists, its pool of large donors was not otherwise that different from past presidential campaigns. And, like other successful candidates, Obama found ways once he gained the office to thank his major financial supporters through invitations to White House events, meetings with the President, and ambassadorships.[c] In light of the expense of running a federal campaign for the presidency or Congress, is it reasonable to expect that small donations can drown out the influence of rich and connected individuals who deliver substantial amounts of money to campaigns? Can the Internet really transform political campaigns,

a. Campaign Finance Institute, *Revised and Updated 2008 Presidential Statistics* (Jan. 2010), http://www.cfinst.org/Press/Releases_tags/10–01–08/Revised_and_Updated_2008_Presidential_Statistics.aspx.

b. Campaign Finance Institute, *Reality Check: Obama Received About the Same Percentage from Small Donors in 2008 as Bush in 2004* (Nov. 24, 2008), http://www.cfinst.org/press/PReleases/08–11–24/Realty_Check_-_Obama_Small_Donors.aspx.

c. See Matthew Mosk, *Democratic Donors Rewarded with W.H. Perks*, Wash. Times, Oct. 28, 2009.

serving as the engine of equalization that *Buckley* rules out for legal change? What challenges does the Internet pose for political campaigns— and what new avenues of reform does it open up?

B. THE BIPARTISAN CAMPAIGN REFORM ACT AND *McCONNELL v. FEDERAL ELECTION COMMISSION*

2. The Bipartisan Campaign Reform Act of 2002

Page 259. Replace the last two sentences of the last paragraph with the following:

Although BCRA would have allowed higher contribution limits to apply to candidates facing self-financed opponents who spend substantial amounts of their own money in their campaigns—a provision called the "million-aire opponent" provision—the Supreme Court struck this down as unconstitutional because it did not further the state's interest in deterring *quid pro quo* corruption. *Davis v. Federal Election Commission*, 128 S.Ct. 2759 (2008). The justification that the provision was required to "equalize the playing field" for candidates who were not personally wealthy was rejected as a revival of the equalization rationale rejected in *Buckley* (casebook, p. 239).

Pages 290–94. Replace Section 3 with the following:

3. The Roberts Court's Change of Course in Campaign Finance Jurisprudence

Although *McConnell* left some questions open, it initially appeared that the issues would be resolved within the *Buckley/McConnell* framework and that the courts would be relatively deferential to legislative decisions regarding the appropriate regulation of campaign contributions. However, two changes in Supreme Court personnel unsettled the jurisprudential landscape. John Roberts replaced Chief Justice Rehnquist, and Samuel Alito replaced Justice Sandra Day O'Connor, one of the authors of the majority opinion in *McConnell*.

In 2007, Wisconsin Right to Life, Inc. (WRTL), a nonprofit ideological advocacy corporation, brought an as-applied challenge to BCRA's rules concerning electioneering communications.[d] During the 30–day period before Wisconsin's 2004 primary election, WRTL planned to run broadcast advertisements telling viewers to contact Senators Feingold and Kohl to urge them to oppose a filibuster of conservative judicial nominees. Because WRTL accepted some contributions from for-profit corporations and the ads it proposed to air met the requirements of § 203, BCRA required that WRTL set up a segregated fund and use that money to pay for the ads.

---

d. For an examination of the Roberts Court's use of as-applied challenges to determine broad questions of election law, see Nathaniel Persily & Jennifer Rosenberg, *Defacing Democracy?: The Changing Nature and Rising Importance of As–Applied Challenges in the Supreme Court's Recent Election Law Decisions*, 93 Minn. L. Rev. 1644 (2009).

In *Federal Election Commission v. Wisconsin Right to Life, Inc.*, 551 U.S. 449 (2007), a majority of the Court agreed with the WRTL that BCRA was unconstitutional as applied to these ads. Chief Justice Roberts and Justice Alito interpreted *McConnell* to allow regulation of issue ads under § 203 only when the communications are the "functional equivalent" of express advocacy. They held that "a court should find that an ad is the functional equivalent of express advocacy only if the ad is susceptible of no reasonable interpretation other than as an appeal to vote for or against a specific candidate." Noting that strict scrutiny demands that a "compelling state interest supports *each application* of a statute restricting speech," the Justices found that BCRA could not be applied in this instance because the concern about *quid pro quo* corruption was not implicated by "genuine" issue ads that are not the functional equivalent of express advocacy. Thus, WRTL could fund them directly with general treasury funds.

The tone of this opinion is markedly different from *McConnell*. The Chief Justice observed at several points in the opinion that the benefit of the doubt must always be provided to "protecting rather than stifling speech." At one point, he noted that "[w]here the First Amendment is implicated, the tie goes to the speaker, not the censor." The Chief Justice strongly admonished those who would regulate such communication: "Enough is enough. * * * To equate WRTL's ads with contributions is to ignore their value as political speech." The result in the case garnered five votes because Justices Kennedy and Thomas joined Justice Scalia's decision in which he argued that this case should have been used to overrule *McConnell* to the extent it had sustained § 203 against facial attack.

A few years later, *McConnell* came under even more serious attack. Citizens United, another ideological nonprofit that accepted a small amount of contributions from for-profit corporations, produced a 90–minute documentary called *Hillary: The Movie*, which it proposed to release on cable video-on-demand channels. The movie was a critical assessment of then-Senator Hillary Clinton (D–N.Y.) and her run for the presidency in 2008. The movie, as well as the ads produced to publicize it, seemed to trigger § 203's requirement that Citizens United use a segregated fund to produce the movie and the ads because all would have been aired within 30 days of the 2008 primary elections. Citizens United had funded the movie directly and thus faced civil and criminal penalties, so it brought an action for declaratory and injunctive relief, arguing that § 203, as well as BCRA's disclosure and disclaimer provisions applying to independent expenditures used for electioneering communications, were unconstitutional as applied to *Hillary* and the surrounding publicity for it.

After losing in federal court, Citizens United appealed to the Supreme Court, which asked for a second round of arguments in an unusual September 2009 argument. The Supreme Court had a new member; Justice Sonia Sotomayor had replaced Justice Souter. The reargument was also noteworthy because it was Solicitor General Elena Kagan's first appearance before the Court; less than a year later, she was nominated to the Supreme Court to replace retiring Justice Stevens. When the Court asked for reargument, it requested supplemental briefs addressing whether it should overrule *Austin v. Michigan Chamber of Commerce* (casebook, pp. 247–50) and the part of *McConnell* dealing with the regulation of electioneering communication (casebook, pp. 270–72). It thus signaled a willingness to revisit the holding of *McConnell* that § 203 was facially constitutional, and not limit its consideration to the as-applied challenge before it. (Note: Section 203 of BCRA amended 2 U.S.C. § 441b, which regulates corporate contributions and independent expenditures for express advocacy. Accordingly, the majority opinion in *Citizens United* refers to § 441b when it considers the regulation of corporate independent expenditures for electioneering communication.)

CITIZENS UNITED v. FEDERAL ELECTION COMMISSION

Supreme Court of the United States, 2010
558 U.S. ___, 130 S.Ct. 876, 175 L.Ed.2d 753

JUSTICE KENNEDY delivered the opinion of the Court, in which THE CHIEF JUSTICE, JUSTICE SCALIA and JUSTICE ALITO, joined, in which JUSTICE THOMAS joined as to all but Part IV, and in which JUSTICES STEVENS, GINSBURG, BREYER, and SOTOMAYOR joined as to Part IV.

Federal law prohibits corporations and unions from using their general treasury funds to make independent expenditures for speech defined as an "electioneering communication" or for speech expressly advocating the election or defeat of a candidate. Limits on electioneering communications were upheld in *McConnell v. Federal Election Comm'n* [casebook, pp. 261–86]. The holding of *McConnell* rested to a large extent on an earlier case, *Austin v. Michigan Chamber of Commerce* [casebook, pp. 247–50]. *Austin* had held that political speech may be banned based on the speaker's corporate identity.

In this case we are asked to reconsider *Austin* and, in effect, *McConnell*. We * * * hold that *stare decisis* does not compel the continued acceptance of *Austin*. The Government may regulate corporate political speech through disclaimer and disclosure requirements, but it may not suppress that speech altogether. * * *

[The Court noted that federal law has long prohibited corporations and unions from using general treasury funds to make direct contributions to candidates or independent expenditures that expressly advocate the election or defeat of a federal candidate. The Court first considered several ways in which it could have decided the case without overruling precedent or reaching the constitutional issues. For example, it had been argued that Citizens United might not meet the test in *WRTL* because *Hillary* should not be considered express advocacy or its functional equivalent; the test provided by *WRTL* was whether the communication is "susceptible of no reasonable interpretation other than as an appeal to vote for or against a specific candidate." But the Court concluded that

Hillary was equivalent to express advocacy: "The movie, in essence, is a feature-length negative advertisement that urges viewers to vote against Senator Clinton for President. In light of historical footage, interviews with persons critical of her, and voiceover narration, the film would be understood by most viewers as an extended criticism of Senator Clinton's character and her fitness for the office of the Presidency."

[Another narrower ground for decision would have been to determine that Citizens United was really the kind of ideological nonprofit that falls outside the ambit of § 441b. This exception, created by the Court in *Federal Election Comm'n v. Massachusetts Citizens for Life*, 479 U.S. 238 (1986), was incorporated into BCRA through statutory interpretation (casebook, p. 260). Although *MCFL*-exempt corporations have been limited to nonprofits that do not receive any financial support from for-profit corporations, both Citizens United and the Government urged the Court to consider expanding the exemption to include nonprofit ideological corporations formed solely to promote political ideas and funded over-whelmingly by individuals. The Court declined to extend the exception because the lawmakers who passed BCRA signaled unambiguously that they intended to adopt the *MCFL* test, which clearly limited its application to nonprofits funded exclusively by individuals. It also noted the difficulty of applying a *de minimis* standard on a case-by-case basis.]

[II.E] As the foregoing analysis confirms, the Court cannot resolve this case on a narrower ground without chilling political speech, speech that is central to the meaning and purpose of the First Amendment. It is not judicial restraint to accept an unsound, narrow argument just so the Court can avoid another argument with broader implications. Indeed, a court would be remiss in performing its duties were it to accept an unsound principle merely to avoid the necessity of making a broader ruling. Here, the lack of a valid basis for an alternative ruling requires full consideration of the continuing effect of the speech suppression upheld in *Austin*.

* * *

When the statute now at issue came before the Court in *McConnell*, both the majority and the dissenting opinions considered the question of its facial validity. The holding and validity of *Austin* were essential to the reasoning of the *McConnell* majority opinion, which upheld BCRA's extension of § 441b. * * * Four Members of the *McConnell* Court would have overruled *Austin*, including Chief Justice Rehnquist, who had joined the Court's opinion in *Austin* but reconsidered that conclusion. * * *

As noted above, Citizens United's narrower arguments are not sustainable under a fair reading of the statute. In the exercise of its judicial responsibility, it is necessary then for the Court to consider the facial validity of § 441b. Any other course of decision would prolong the substantial, nation-wide chilling effect caused by § 441b's prohibitions on corporate expenditures. * * *

[S]ubstantial time would be required to bring clarity to the application of the statutory provision on these points in order to avoid any chilling effect caused by some improper interpretation. It is well known that the public begins to concentrate on elections only in the weeks immediately before they are held. There are short timeframes in which speech can have influence. The need or relevance of the speech will often first be apparent at this stage in the campaign. The decision to speak is made in the heat of political campaigns, when speakers react to messages conveyed by others. A speaker's ability to engage in political speech that could have a chance of persuading voters is stifled if the speaker must first commence a protracted lawsuit. By the time the lawsuit concludes, the election will be over and the litigants in most cases will have neither the incentive nor, perhaps, the resources to carry on, even if they could establish that the case is not moot because the issue is "capable of repetition, yet evading review." Here, Citizens United decided to litigate its case to the end. Today, Citizens United finally learns, two years after the fact, whether it could have spoken during the 2008 Presidential primary—long after the opportunity to persuade primary voters has passed.

[An additional factor] is the primary importance of speech itself to the integrity of the election process. As additional rules are created for regulating political speech, any speech arguably within their reach is chilled. Campaign finance regulations now impose "unique and complex rules" on "71 distinct entities." Brief for Seven Former Chairmen of FEC et al. as *Amici Curiae* 11–12. These entities are subject to separate rules for 33 different types of political speech. The FEC has adopted 568 pages of regulations, 1,278 pages of explanations and justifications for those regulations, and 1,771 advisory opinions since 1975. In fact, after this Court in *WRTL* adopted an objective "appeal to vote" test for determining whether a communication was the functional equivalent of express advocacy, the FEC adopted a two-part, 11–factor balancing test to implement *WRTL*'s ruling.

This regulatory scheme may not be a prior restraint on speech in the strict sense of that term, for prospective speakers are not compelled by law to seek an advisory opinion from the FEC before the speech takes place. As a practical matter, however, given the complexity of the regulations and the deference courts show to administrative determinations, a speaker who wants to avoid threats of criminal liability and the heavy costs of defending against FEC enforcement must ask a governmental agency for prior permission to speak. * * * Because the FEC's "business is to censor, there inheres the danger that [it] may well be less responsive than a court—part of an independent branch of government—to the constitutionally protected interests in free expression." *Freedman v. Maryland*, 380 U.S. 51, 57–58 (1965). * * *

This is precisely what *WRTL* sought to avoid. *WRTL* said that First Amendment standards "must eschew 'the open-ended rough-and-tumble of factors,' which 'invit[es] complex argument in a trial court and a virtually inevitable appeal.'" Yet, the FEC has created a regime that allows it to select what political speech is safe for public consumption by applying ambiguous tests. If parties want to avoid litigation and the possibility of civil and criminal penalties, they must either refrain from speaking or ask the FEC to issue an advisory opinion approving of the political speech in question. Government officials pore over each word of a text to see if, in their judgment, it accords with the 11–factor test they have promulgated. This is an unprecedented governmental intervention into the realm of speech.

The ongoing chill upon speech that is beyond all doubt protected makes it necessary in this case to invoke the earlier precedents that a statute which chills speech can and must be invalidated where its facial invalidity has been demonstrated. For these reasons we find it necessary to reconsider *Austin*.

[III]   * * *

The law before us is an outright ban [of political speech], backed by criminal sanctions. Section 441b makes it a felony for all corporations— including nonprofit advocacy corporations—either to expressly advocate the election or defeat of candidates or to broadcast electioneering communications within 30 days of a primary election and 60 days of a general election. Thus, the following acts would all be felonies under § 441b: The Sierra Club runs an ad, within the crucial phase of 60 days before the general election, that exhorts the public to disapprove of a Congressman who favors logging in national forests; the National Rifle Association publishes a book urging the public to vote for the challenger because the incumbent U.S. Senator supports a handgun ban; and the American Civil Liberties Union creates a Web site telling the public to vote for a Presidential candidate in light of that candidate's defense of free speech. These prohibitions are classic examples of censorship.

Section 441b is a ban on corporate speech notwithstanding the fact that a PAC created by a corporation can still speak. A PAC is a separate association from the corporation. So the PAC exemption from § 441b's expenditure ban does not allow corporations to speak. Even if a PAC could somehow allow a corporation to speak—and it does not—the option to form PACs does not alleviate the First Amendment problems with § 441b. PACs are burdensome alternatives; they are expensive to administer and subject to extensive regulations. For example, every PAC must appoint a treasurer, forward donations to the treasurer promptly, keep detailed records of the identities of the persons making donations, preserve receipts for three years, and file an organization statement and report changes to this information within 10 days. * * *

Section 441b's prohibition on corporate independent expenditures is thus a ban on speech. * * * If § 441b applied to individuals, no one would believe that it is merely a time, place, or manner restriction on speech. Its purpose and effect are to silence entities whose voices the Government deems to be suspect. * * *

Premised on mistrust of governmental power, the First Amendment stands against attempts to disfavor certain subjects or viewpoints. Prohibited, too, are restrictions distinguishing among different speakers, allowing speech by some but not others. As instruments to censor, these categories are interrelated: Speech restrictions based on the identity of the speaker are all too often simply a means to control content. * * *

[The Court cited a long line of precedents holding that corporations are protected by the First Amendment and that the protection extends to corporate political speech. Nonetheless, direct contributions to candidates by corporations have been banned since the latter part of the 19th century, and in 1947 Congress prohibited independent expenditures in candidate elections by corporations and unions. After the Court in *Buckley* invalidated FECA's restriction on independent expenditures in federal elections (casebook, pp. 238–40), Congress enacted a prohibition on the use of general treasury funds of corporations or unions for independent expenditures funding express advocacy. Subsequent Supreme Court cases dealt with corporate expenditures in state ballot measure campaigns. In *First National Bank of Boston v. Bellotti*, 435 U.S. 765 (1978), the Court struck down a state ban on the use of corporate treasury funds for such expenditures, resting on "the principle that the Government lacks the power to ban corporations from speaking." The next time the Court considered corporate political speech was in *Austin*. "To bypass *Buckley* and *Bellotti*, the *Austin* Court identified a new governmental interest in limiting political speech: an antidistortion interest."]

[III.B] The Court is thus confronted with conflicting lines of precedent: a pre-*Austin* line that forbids restrictions on political speech based on the speaker's corporate identity and a post-*Austin* line that permits them. * * *

In its defense of the corporate-speech restrictions in § 441b, the Government notes the antidistortion rationale on which *Austin* and its progeny rest in part, yet it all but abandons reliance upon it. It argues instead that two other compelling interests support *Austin*'s holding that corporate expenditure restrictions are constitutional: an anticorruption interest, and a shareholder-protection interest. We consider the three points in turn.

* * * [First,] *Austin* sought to defend the antidistortion rationale as a means to prevent corporations from obtaining "an unfair advantage in the political marketplace" by using "resources amassed in the economic marketplace." But *Buckley* rejected the premise that the Government has an interest "in equalizing the relative ability of individuals and groups to influence the outcome of elections." * * * The rule that political speech cannot be limited based on a speaker's wealth is a necessary consequence of the premise that the First Amendment generally prohibits the suppression of political speech based on the speaker's identity.

Either as support for its antidistortion rationale or as a further argument, the *Austin* majority undertook to distinguish wealthy individuals from corporations on the ground that "[s]tate law grants corporations special advantages—such as limited liability, perpetual life, and favorable treatment of the accumulation and distribution of assets." This does not suffice, however, to allow laws prohibiting speech. "It is rudimentary that the State cannot exact as the price of those special advantages the forfeiture of First Amendment rights." *Austin* (SCALIA, J., dissenting). * * *

Austin interferes with the "open marketplace" of ideas protected by the *First Amendment*. It permits the Government to ban the political speech of millions of associations of citizens. See *Statistics of Income* 2 (5.8 million for-profit corporations filed 2006 tax returns). Most of these are small corporations without large amounts of wealth. See Supp. Brief for Chamber of Commerce of the United States of America as *Amicus Curiae* 1, 3 (96% of the 3 million businesses that belong to the U.S. Chamber of Commerce have fewer than 100 employees); M. Keightley, Congressional Research Service Report for Congress, *Business Organizational Choices: Taxation and Responses to Legislative Changes* 10 (2009) (more than 75% of corporations whose income is taxed under federal law * * * have less than $1 million in receipts per year). This fact belies the Government's argument that the statute is justified on the ground that it prevents the "distorting effects of immense aggregations of wealth." *Austin*. It is not even aimed at amassed wealth.

The censorship we now confront is vast in its reach. The Government has "muffle[d] the voices that best represent the most significant segments of the economy." *McConnell* (opinion of SCALIA, J.). * * * By suppressing the speech of manifold corporations, both for-profit and nonprofit, the Government prevents their voices and viewpoints from reaching the public and advising voters on which persons or entities are hostile to their interests. Factions will necessarily form in our Republic, but the remedy of "destroying the liberty" of some factions is "worse than the disease." *The Federalist No. 10* (J. Madison). Factions should be checked by permitting them all to speak, and by entrusting the people to judge what is true and what is false.

The purpose and effect of this law is to prevent corporations, including small and nonprofit corporations, from presenting both facts and opinions to the public. * * * Corporate executives and employees counsel Members of Congress and Presidential administrations on many issues, as a matter of routine and often in private. An *amici* brief filed on behalf of Montana and 25 other States notes that lobbying and corporate communications with elected officials occur on a regular basis. When that phenomenon is coupled with § 441b, the result is that smaller or nonprofit corporations cannot raise a voice to object when other corporations, including those with vast wealth, are cooperating with the Government. That cooperation may sometimes be voluntary, or it may be at the demand of a Government official who uses his or her authority, influence, and power to threaten corporations to support the Government's policies. Those kinds of interactions are often unknown and unseen. The speech that § 441b forbids, though, is public, and all can judge its content and purpose. References to massive corporate treasuries should not mask the real operation of this law. Rhetoric ought not obscure reality.

* * *

When Government seeks to use its full power, including the criminal law, to command where a person may get his or her information or what distrusted source he or she may not hear, it uses censorship to control thought. This is unlawful. The First Amendment confirms the freedom to think for ourselves.

[The Court turned then to the argument that § 441b was designed to prevent corruption and its appearance. It relied on the analysis in *Buckley* to hold that independent expenditures, not coordinated or arranged with a candidate, do not sufficiently implicate concerns about *quid pro quo* corruption to allow the restriction at issue in *Citizens United*. Finally, it addressed the argument that corporate independent expenditures can be limited because of a state interest "in protecting dissenting shareholders from being compelled to fund corporate political speech."]

[With regard to this interest of shareholder protection,] the statute is both underinclusive and overinclusive. As to the first, if Congress had been seeking to protect dissenting shareholders, it would not have banned corporate speech in only certain media within 30 or 60 days before an election. A dissenting shareholder's interests would be implicated by speech in any media at any time. As to the second, the statute is overinclusive because it covers all corporations, including nonprofit corporations and for-profit corporations with only single shareholders. * * *

[III.C] * * * For the reasons above, it must be concluded that *Austin* was not well reasoned. The Government defends *Austin*, relying almost entirely on "the quid pro quo interest, the corruption interest or the shareholder interest," and not *Austin*'s expressed antidistortion rationale. When neither party defends the reasoning of a precedent, the principle of adhering to that precedent through *stare decisis* is diminished. * * *

Austin is undermined by experience since its announcement. Political speech is so ingrained in our culture that speakers find ways to circumvent campaign finance laws. Our Nation's speech dynamic is changing, and informative voices should not have to circumvent onerous restrictions to exercise their First Amendment rights. Speakers have become adept at presenting citizens with sound bites, talking points, and scripted messages that dominate the 24–hour news cycle. Corporations, like individuals, do not have monolithic views. On certain topics corporations may possess valuable expertise, leaving them the best equipped to point out errors or fallacies in speech of all sorts, including the speech of candidates and elected officials.

Rapid changes in technology—and the creative dynamic inherent in the concept of free expression—counsel against upholding a law that restricts political speech in certain media or by certain speakers. Today, 30–second television ads may be the most effective way to convey a political message. Soon, however, it may be that Internet sources, such as blogs and social networking Web sites, will provide citizens with significant information about political candidates and issues. Yet, § 441b would seem to ban a blog post expressly advocating the election or defeat of a candidate if that blog were created with corporate funds. The First Amendment does not permit Congress to make these categorical distinctions based on the corporate identity of the speaker and the content of the political speech.

No serious reliance interests are at stake. As the Court stated in *Payne v. Tennessee,* 501 U.S. 808, 828 (1991), reliance interests are important considerations in property and contract cases, where parties may have acted in conformance with existing legal rules in order to conduct transactions. Here, though, parties have been prevented from acting—corporations have been banned from making independent expenditures. Legislatures may have enacted bans on corporate expenditures believing that those bans were constitutional. This is not a compelling interest for *stare decisis*. If it were, legislative acts could prevent us from overruling our own precedents, thereby interfering with our duty "to say what the law is." *Marbury v. Madison*, 5 U.S. 137, 1 Cranch 137, 177 (1803).

Due consideration leads to this conclusion: *Austin* should be and now is overruled. We return to the principle established in *Buckley* and *Bellotti* that the Government may not suppress political speech on the basis of the speaker's corporate identity. No sufficient governmental interest justifies limits on the political speech of nonprofit or for-profit corporations.

    * * *

Given our conclusion we are further required to overrule the part of *McConnell* that upheld BCRA § 203's extension of § 441b's restrictions on corporate independent expenditures. The *McConnell* Court relied on the antidistortion interest recognized in *Austin* to uphold a greater restriction on speech than the restriction upheld in *Austin*, and we have found this interest unconvincing and insufficient. This part of *McConnell* is now overruled.

[The Court then upheld BCRA's disclosure and disclaimer provisions as applied to *Hillary* and the ads for the movie. BCRA requires that electioneering communications funded by entities other than candidates include a disclaimer identifying the person or group responsible for the content of the communication, and that any entity spending more than $10,000 on electioneering communications within a calendar year must file a disclosure statement with the FEC. The Court found that disclosure served the compelling state interest of providing the electorate with information necessary to evaluate the arguments and to avoid confusion about who is behind the communications. It approved of applying disclosure provisions to a wide array of political communication, not just express advocacy and its functional equivalent. It found that "the informational interest alone is sufficient to justify" applying BCRA's disclosure provisions to the movie and ads produced by Citizens United. It rejected Citizens United's argument that disclosure could subject its donors to threats or harassment because there was no such evidence of retaliation even though Citizens United has disclosed its donors publicly for years.]

[V]   When word concerning the plot of the movie *Mr. Smith Goes to Washington* reached the circles of Government, some officials sought, by persuasion, to discourage its distribution. Under *Austin*, though, officials could have done more than discourage its distribution—they could have banned the film. After all, it, like *Hillary,* was speech funded by a corporation that was critical of Members of Congress. *Mr. Smith Goes to Washington* may be fiction and caricature; but fiction and caricature can be a powerful force.

Modern day movies, television comedies, or skits on Youtube.com might portray public officials or public policies in unflattering ways. Yet if a covered transmission during the blackout period creates the background for candidate endorsement or opposition, a felony occurs solely because a corporation, other than an exempt media corporation, has made the "purchase, payment, distribution, loan, advance, deposit, or gift of money or anything of value" in order to engage in political speech. 2 U.S.C. § 431(9)(A)(i). Speech would be suppressed in the realm where its necessity is most evident: in the public dialogue preceding a real election. Governments are often hostile to speech, but under our law and our tradition it seems stranger than fiction for our Government to make this political speech a crime. Yet this is the statute's purpose and design.

Some members of the public might consider *Hillary* to be insightful and instructive; some might find it to be neither high art nor a fair discussion on how to set the Nation's course; still others simply might suspend judgment on these points but decide to think more about issues and candidates. Those choices and assessments, however, are not for the Government to make. "The First Amendment underwrites the freedom to experiment and to create in the realm of thought and speech. Citizens must be free to use new forms, and new forums, for the expression of ideas. The civic discourse belongs to the people, and the Government may not prescribe the means used to conduct it." *McConnell* (opinion of KENNEDY, J.).

* * *

It is so ordered.

[The concurrence of CHIEF JUSTICE ROBERTS is omitted. His main focus was to reconcile the decision to overrule *Austin* and parts of *McConnell* with principles of judicial restraint and *stare decisis*. He characterized *Austin* as an aberration, departing from the "robust protections" provided to political speech, including that of corporations, before. He also understood *Austin* to be justified by egalitarian principles, which could be used to allow much more restrictive regulation of political spending for speech by more than just corporations. It is thus "uniquely destabilizing because it threatens to subvert our Court's decisions even outside the particular context of corporate express advocacy." The concurrence of JUSTICE SCALIA is also omitted.]

JUSTICE STEVENS, with whom JUSTICE GINSBURG, JUSTICE BREYER, and JUSTICE SOTOMAYOR join, concurring in part [with respect to the disclosure provisions] and dissenting in part.

The real issue in this case concerns how, not if, the appellant may finance its electioneering. Citizens United is a wealthy nonprofit corporation that runs a political action committee (PAC) with millions of dollars in assets. Under the Bipartisan Campaign Reform Act of 2002 (BCRA), it could have used those assets to televise and promote *Hillary: The Movie* wherever and whenever it wanted to. It also could have spent unrestricted sums to broadcast *Hillary* at any time other than the 30 days before the last primary election. Neither Citizens United's nor any other corporation's speech has been "banned." All that the parties dispute is whether Citizens United had a right to use the funds in its general treasury to pay for broadcasts during the 30–day period. The notion that the First Amendment dictates an affirmative answer to that question is, in my judgment, profoundly misguided. Even more misguided is the notion that the Court must rewrite the law relating to campaign expenditures by *for-profit* corporations and unions to decide this case.

The basic premise underlying the Court's ruling is its iteration, and constant reiteration, of the proposition that the First Amendment bars regulatory distinctions based on a speaker's identity, including its "identity" as a corporation. While that glittering generality has rhetorical appeal, it is not a correct statement of the law. Nor does it tell us when a corporation may engage in electioneering that some of its shareholders oppose. It does not even resolve the specific question whether Citizens United may be required to finance some of its messages with the money in its PAC. The conceit that corporations must be treated identically to natural persons in the political sphere is not only inaccurate but also inadequate to justify the Court's disposition of this case.

In the context of election to public office, the distinction between corporate and human speakers is significant. Although they make enormous contributions to our society, corporations are not actually members of it. They cannot vote or run for office. Because they may be managed and controlled by nonresidents, their interests may conflict in fundamental respects with the interests of eligible voters. The financial resources, legal structure, and instrumental orientation of corporations raise legitimate concerns about their role in the electoral process. Our lawmakers have a compelling constitutional basis, if not also a democratic duty, to take measures designed to guard against the potentially deleterious effects of corporate spending in local and national races.

The majority's approach to corporate electioneering marks a dramatic break from our past. Congress has placed special limitations on campaign spending by corporations ever since the passage of the Tillman Act in 1907, ch. 420, 34 Stat. 864. * * * The Court today rejects a century of history when it treats the distinction between corporate and individual campaign spending as an invidious novelty born of *Austin v. Michigan Chamber of Commerce.* * * *

[The dissent takes strong issue with the decision of the Court to overrule its precedents, thereby deciding the case "on a basis relinquished below, not included in the questions presented to us by the litigants, and argued here only in response to the Court's invitation. * * * Our colleagues' suggestion that 'we are asked to reconsider *Austin* and, in effect, *McConnell*,' would be more accurate if rephrased to state that 'we have asked ourselves' to reconsider those cases."]

* * *

We have recognized that "*[s]tare decisis* has special force when legislators or citizens 'have acted in reliance on a previous decision, for in this instance overruling the decision would dislodge settled rights and expectations or require an extensive legislative response.' " *Hubbard v. United States,* 514 U.S. 695, 714 (1995). *Stare decisis* protects not only personal rights involving property or contract but also the ability of the elected branches to shape their laws in an effective and coherent fashion. Today's decision takes away a power that we have long permitted these branches to exercise. State legislatures have relied on their authority to regulate corporate electioneering, confirmed in *Austin*, for more than a century. The Federal Congress has relied on this authority for a comparable stretch of time, and it specifically relied on *Austin* throughout the years it spent developing and debating BCRA. The total record it compiled was *100,000 pages* long. Pulling out the rug beneath Congress after affirming the constitutionality of § 203 six years ago shows great disrespect for a coequal branch.

* * *

[III] The novelty of the Court's procedural dereliction and its approach to *stare decisis* is matched by the novelty of its ruling on the merits. The ruling rests on several premises. First, the Court claims that *Austin* and *McConnell* have "banned" corporate speech. Second, it claims that the First Amendment precludes regulatory distinctions based on speaker identity, including the speaker's identity as a corporation. Third, it claims that *Austin* and *McConnell* were radical outliers in our First Amendment tradition and our campaign finance jurisprudence. Each of these claims is wrong.

The So–Called "Ban"

Pervading the Court's analysis is the ominous image of a "categorical ba[n]" on corporate speech. Indeed, the majority invokes the specter of a "ban" on nearly every page of its opinion. This characterization is highly misleading, and needs to be corrected.

In fact it already has been. Our cases have repeatedly pointed out that, "[c]ontrary to the [majority's] critical assumptions," the statutes upheld in *Austin* and *McConnell* do "not impose an *absolute* ban on all forms of corporate political spending." *Austin;* see also *McConnell.* For starters, both statutes provide exemptions for PACs, separate segregated funds established by a corporation for political purposes. "The ability to form and administer separate segregated funds," we observed in *McConnell*, "has provided corporations and unions with a constitutionally sufficient opportunity to engage in express advocacy. That has been this Court's unanimous view."

    * * * Administering a PAC entails some administrative burden, but so does complying with the disclaimer, disclosure, and reporting requirements that the Court today upholds, and no one has suggested that the burden is severe for a sophisticated for-profit corporation. To the extent the majority is worried about this issue, it is important to keep in mind that we have no record to show how substantial the burden really is, just the majority's own unsupported factfinding. Like all other natural persons, every shareholder of every corporation remains entirely free under *Austin* and *McConnell* to do however much electioneering she pleases outside of the corporate form. The owners of a "mom & pop" store can simply place ads in their own names, rather than the store's. If ideologically aligned individuals wish to make unlimited expenditures through the corporate form, they may utilize an *MCFL* organization that has policies in place to avoid becoming a conduit for business or union interests.
    * * *

So let us be clear: Neither *Austin* nor *McConnell* held or implied that corporations may be silenced; the FEC is not a "censor"; and in the years since these cases were decided, corporations have continued to play a major role in the national dialogue. Laws such as § 203 target a class of communications that is especially likely to corrupt the political process, that is at least one degree removed from the views of individual citizens, and that may not even reflect the views of those who pay for it. Such laws burden political speech, and that is always a serious matter, demanding careful scrutiny. But the majority's incessant talk of a "ban" aims at a straw man.

Identity–Based Distinctions

    The second pillar of the Court's opinion is its assertion that "the Government cannot restrict political speech based on the speaker's . . . identity." * * * Like its paeans to unfettered discourse, the Court's denunciation of identity-based distinctions may have rhetorical appeal but it obscures reality.
    * * *

The election context is distinctive in many ways, and the Court, of course, is right that the First Amendment closely guards political speech. But in this context, too, the authority of legislatures to enact viewpoint-neutral regulations based on content and identity is well settled. We have, for example, allowed state-run broadcasters to exclude independent candidates from televised debates. *Arkansas Ed. Television Comm'n v. Forbes,* 523 U.S. 666 (1998). We have upheld statutes that prohibit the distribution or display of campaign materials near a polling place. *Burson v. Freeman,* 504 U.S. 191 (1992). * * *

The same logic applies to this case with additional force because it is the identity of corporations, rather than individuals, that the Legislature has taken into account. As we have unanimously observed, legislatures are entitled to decide "that the special characteristics of the corporate structure require particularly careful regulation" in an electoral context. *Federal Election Commission v. National Right to Work Committee,* 459 U.S. 197, 209–10 (1982). Not only has the distinctive potential of corporations to corrupt the electoral process long been recognized, but * * * [c]ampaign finance distinctions based on corporate identity tend to be less worrisome, * * * because the "speakers" are not natural persons, much less members of our political community, and the governmental interests are of the highest order. Furthermore, when corporations, as a class, are distinguished from noncorporations, as a class, there is a lesser risk that regulatory distinctions will reflect invidious discrimination or political favoritism.

If taken seriously, our colleagues' assumption that the identity of a speaker has *no* relevance to the Government's ability to regulate political speech would lead to some remarkable conclusions. Such an assumption would have accorded the propaganda broadcasts to our troops by "Tokyo Rose" during World War II the same protection as speech by Allied commanders. More pertinently, it would appear to afford the same protection to multinational corporations controlled by foreigners as to individual Americans: To do otherwise, after all, could "enhance the relative voice" of some (*i.e.,* humans) over others (*i.e.,* nonhumans). Under the majority's view, I suppose it may be a First Amendment problem that corporations are not permitted to vote, given that voting is, among other things, a form of speech.

* * *

Our First Amendment Tradition

A third fulcrum of the Court's opinion is the idea that *Austin* and *McConnell* are radical outliers, "aberration[s]," in our First Amendment tradition. The Court has it exactly backwards. It is today's holding that is the radical departure from what had been settled First Amendment law. * * *

* * * At the federal level, the express distinction between corporate and individual political spending on elections stretches back to 1907, when Congress passed the Tillman Act, ch. 420, 34 Stat. 864, banning all corporate contributions to candidates. The Senate Report on the legislation observed that "[t]he evils of the use of [corporate] money in connec-

tion with political elections are so generally recognized that the committee deems it unnecessary to make any argument in favor of the general purpose of this measure. It is in the interest of good government and calculated to promote purity in the selection of public officials." * * *

Over the years, the limitations on corporate political spending have been modified in a number of ways, as Congress responded to changes in the American economy and political practices that threatened to displace the commonweal. * * * The Taft–Hartley Act of 1947 is of special significance for this case. In that Act passed more than 60 years ago, Congress extended the prohibition on corporate support of candidates to cover not only direct contributions, but independent expenditures as well. Labor Management Relations Act, 1947, § 304, 61 Stat. 159. * * *

By the time Congress passed FECA in 1971, the bar on corporate contributions and expenditures had become such an accepted part of federal campaign finance regulation that when a large number of plaintiffs, including several nonprofit corporations, challenged virtually every aspect of the Act in *Buckley,* no one even bothered to argue that the bar as such was unconstitutional. *Buckley* famously (or infamously) distinguished direct contributions from independent expenditures, but its silence on corporations only reinforced the understanding that corporate expenditures could be treated differently from individual expenditures. "Since our decision in *Buckley*, Congress' power to prohibit corporations and unions from using funds in their treasuries to finance advertisements expressly advocating the election or defeat of candidates in federal elections has been firmly embedded in our law." *McConnell.*

* * *

[IV]   Having explained why this is not an appropriate case in which to revisit *Austin* and *McConnell* and why these decisions sit perfectly well with "First Amendment principles," I come at last to the interests that are at stake. The majority recognizes that *Austin* and *McConnell* may be defended on anticorruption, antidistortion, and shareholder protection rationales. * * *

The Anticorruption Interest

Undergirding the majority's approach to the merits is the claim that the only "sufficiently important governmental interest in preventing corruption or the appearance of corruption" is one that is "limited to *quid pro quo* corruption." This is the same "crabbed view of corruption" that was * * * squarely rejected by the Court in [*McConnell*]. While it is true that we have not always spoken about corruption in a clear or consistent voice, the approach taken by the majority cannot be right, in my judgment. It disregards our constitutional history and the fundamental demands of a democratic society.

* * *

Quid Pro Quo *Corruption*

* * * Even in the cases that have construed the anticorruption interest most narrowly, we have never suggested that such *quid pro quo* debts must take the form of outright vote buying or bribes, which have long been distinct crimes. Rather, they encompass the myriad ways in which outside parties may induce an officeholder to confer a legislative benefit in direct response to, or anticipation of, some outlay of money the parties have made or will make on behalf of the officeholder. * * * A democracy cannot function effectively when its constituent members believe laws are being bought and sold.

* * * Corporations, as a class, tend to be more attuned to the complexities of the legislative process and more directly affected by tax and appropriations measures that receive little public scrutiny; they also have vastly more money with which to try to buy access and votes. See Supp. Brief for Appellee 17 (stating that the Fortune 100 companies earned revenues of $13.1 trillion during the last election cycle). Business corporations must engage the political process in instrumental terms if they are to maximize shareholder value. The unparalleled resources, professional lobbyists, and single-minded focus they bring to this effort * * * make *quid pro quo* corruption and its appearance inherently more likely when they (or their conduits or trade groups) spend unrestricted sums on elections.

* * *

The majority appears to think it decisive that the BCRA record does not contain "direct examples of votes being exchanged for . . . expenditures." It would have been quite remarkable if Congress had created a record detailing such behavior by its own Members. Proving that a specific vote was exchanged for a specific expenditure has always been next to impossible: Elected officials have diverse motivations, and no one will acknowledge that he sold a vote. * * * The influx of unlimited corporate money into the electoral realm also creates new opportunities for the mirror image of *quid pro quo* deals: threats, both explicit and implicit. Starting today, corporations with large war chests to deploy on electioneering may find democratically elected bodies becoming much more attuned to their interests. * * *

Austin and Corporate Expenditures

Just as the majority gives short shrift to the general societal interests at stake in campaign finance regulation, it also overlooks the distinctive considerations raised by the regulation of *corporate* expenditures. The majority fails to appreciate that *Austin*'s antidistortion rationale is itself an anticorruption rationale, tied to the special concerns raised by corporations. Understood properly, "antidistortion" is simply a variant on the classic governmental interest in protecting against improper influences on officeholders that debilitate the democratic process. It is manifestly not just an "equalizing" ideal in disguise.

1. *Antidistortion*

The fact that corporations are different from human beings might seem to need no elaboration, except that the majority opinion almost completely elides it. *Austin* set forth some of the basic differences. Unlike natural persons, corporations have "limited liability" for their owners and managers, "perpetual life," separation of ownership and control, "and favorable treatment of the accumulation and distribution of assets . . . that enhance their ability to attract capital and to deploy their resources in ways that maximize the return on their shareholders' investments." * * * "[T]he resources in the treasury of a business corporation," furthermore, "are not an indication of popular support for the corporation's political ideas." *Austin*. "They reflect instead the economically motivated decisions of investors and customers. The availability of these resources may make a corporation a formidable political presence, even though the power of the corporation may be no reflection of the power of its ideas." *Austin*.

It might also be added that corporations have no consciences, no beliefs, no feelings, no thoughts, no desires. Corporations help structure and facilitate the activities of human beings, to be sure, and their "personhood" often serves as a useful legal fiction. But they are not themselves members of "We the People" by whom and for whom our Constitution was established.

These basic points help explain why corporate electioneering is not only more likely to impair compelling governmental interests, but also why restrictions on that electioneering are less likely to encroach upon First Amendment freedoms. * * * Corporate speech * * * is derivative speech, speech by proxy. A regulation such as BCRA § 203 may affect the way in which individuals disseminate certain messages through the corporate form, but it does not prevent anyone from speaking in his or her own voice. * * *

It is an interesting question "who" is even speaking when a business corporation places an advertisement that endorses or attacks a particular candidate. Presumably it is not the customers or employees, who typically have no say in such matters. It cannot realistically be said to be the shareholders, who tend to be far removed from the day-to-day decisions of the firm and whose political preferences may be opaque to management. Perhaps the officers or directors of the corporation have the best claim to be the ones speaking, except their fiduciary duties generally prohibit them from using corporate funds for personal ends. Some individuals associated with the corporation must make the decision to place the ad, but the idea that these individuals are thereby fostering their self-expression or cultivating their critical faculties is fanciful. It is entirely possible that the corporation's electoral message will *conflict* with their personal convictions. Take away the ability to use general treasury funds for some of those ads, and no one's autonomy, dignity, or political equality has been impinged upon in the least.

* * *

In this transactional spirit, some corporations have affirmatively urged Congress to place limits on their electioneering communications. These corporations fear that officeholders will shake them down for supportive ads, that they will have to spend increasing sums on elections in an ever-escalating arms race with their competitors, and that public trust in business will be eroded. A system that effectively forces corporations to use their shareholders' money both to maintain access to, and to avoid retribution from, elected officials may ultimately prove more harmful than beneficial to many corporations. It can impose a kind of implicit tax.

* * * Recognizing the weakness of a speaker-based critique of *Austin*, the Court places primary emphasis not on the corporation's right to electioneer, but rather on the listener's interest in hearing what every possible speaker may have to say. The Court's central argument is that laws such as § 203 have "deprived [the electorate] of information, knowledge and opinion vital to its function," and this, in turn, "interferes with the 'open marketplace' of ideas protected by the First Amendment."

There are many flaws in this argument. If the overriding concern depends on the interests of the audience, surely the public's perception of the value of corporate speech should be given important weight. That perception today is the same as it was a century ago when Theodore Roosevelt delivered the speeches to Congress that, in time, led to the limited prohibition on corporate campaign expenditures that is overruled today. The distinctive threat to democratic integrity posed by corporate domination of politics was recognized at "the inception of the republic" and "has been a persistent theme in American political life" ever since. Regan, [Corporate Speech and Civic Virtue, in Debating Democracy's Discontent 289, 302 (A. Allen & M. Regan eds., 1998)]. It is only certain Members of this Court, not the listeners themselves, who have agitated for more corporate electioneering.

* * *

In addition to this immediate drowning out of noncorporate voices, there may be deleterious effects that follow soon thereafter. * * * When citizens turn on their televisions and radios before an election and hear only corporate electioneering, they may lose faith in their capacity, as citizens, to influence public policy. A Government captured by corporate interests, they may come to believe, will be neither responsive to their needs nor willing to give their views a fair hearing. The predictable result is cynicism and disenchantment: an increased perception that large spenders "call the tune" and a reduced "willingness of voters to take part in democratic governance." *McConnell*. To the extent that corporations are allowed to exert undue influence in electoral races, the speech of the eventual winners of those races may also be chilled. Politicians who fear that a certain corporation can make or break their reelection chances may be cowed into silence about that corporation. * * * At the least, I stress again, a legislature is entitled to credit these concerns and to take tailored measures in response.

* * *

None of this is to suggest that corporations can or should be denied an opportunity to participate in election campaigns or in any other public forum (much less that a work of art such as *Mr. Smith Goes to Washington* may be banned), or to deny that some corporate speech may contribute significantly to public debate. What it shows, however, is that *Austin's* "concern about corporate domination of the political process" reflects more than a concern to protect governmental interests outside of the First Amendment. It also reflects a concern to *facilitate* First Amendment values by preserving some breathing room around the electoral "marketplace" of ideas, the marketplace in which the actual people of this Nation determine how they will govern themselves. The majority seems oblivious to the simple truth that laws such as § 203 do not merely pit the anticorruption interest against the First Amendment, but also pit competing First Amendment values against each other. There are, to be sure, serious concerns with any effort to balance the First Amendment rights of speakers against the First Amendment rights of listeners. But when the speakers in question are not real people and when the appeal to "First Amendment principles" depends almost entirely on the listeners' perspective, it becomes necessary to consider how listeners will actually be affected.

* * *

The Court's blinkered and aphoristic approach to the *First Amendment* may well promote corporate power at the cost of the individual and collective self-expression the Amendment was meant to serve. It will undoubtedly cripple the ability of ordinary citizens, Congress, and the States to adopt even limited measures to protect against corporate domination of the electoral process. Americans may be forgiven if they do not feel the Court has advanced the cause of self-government today.

2. *Shareholder Protection*

There is yet another way in which laws such as § 203 can serve First Amendment values. Interwoven with *Austin's* concern to protect the integrity of the electoral process is a concern to protect the rights of shareholders from a kind of coerced speech: electioneering expenditures that do not "reflec[t] [their] support." When corporations use general treasury funds to praise or attack a particular candidate for office, it is the shareholders, as the residual claimants, who are effectively footing the bill. Those shareholders who disagree with the corporation's electoral message may find their financial investments being used to undermine their political convictions.

The PAC mechanism, by contrast, helps assure that those who pay for an electioneering communication actually support its content and that managers do not use general treasuries to advance personal agendas. * * *

The Court dismisses this interest on the ground that abuses of shareholder money can be corrected "through the procedures of corporate democracy," and, it seems, through Internet-based disclosures.[76] I fail to understand how this addresses the concerns of dissenting union members, who will also be affected by today's ruling, and I fail to understand why the Court is so confident in these mechanisms. By "corporate democracy," presumably the Court means the rights of shareholders to vote and to bring derivative suits for breach of fiduciary duty. In practice, however, many corporate lawyers will tell you that "these rights are so limited as to be almost nonexistent," given the internal authority wielded by boards and managers and the expansive protections afforded by the business judgment rule. Blair & Stout, [A Team Production Theory of Corporate Law, 85 Va. L. Rev. 247, 320 (1999)]. Modern technology may help make it easier to track corporate activity, including electoral advocacy, but it is utopian to believe that it solves the problem. * * *

[V] Today's decision is backwards in many senses. It elevates the majority's agenda over the litigants' submissions, facial attacks over as-applied claims, broad constitutional theories over narrow statutory grounds, individual dissenting opinions over precedential holdings, assertion over tradition, absolutism over empiricism, rhetoric over reality. Our colleagues have arrived at the conclusion that *Austin* must be overruled and that § 203 is facially unconstitutional only after mischaracterizing both the reach and rationale of those authorities, and after bypassing or ignoring rules of judicial restraint used to cabin the Court's lawmaking power. Their conclusion that the societal interest in avoiding corruption and the appearance of corruption does not provide an adequate justification for regulating corporate expenditures on candidate elections relies on an incorrect description of that interest, along with a failure to acknowledge the relevance of established facts and the considered judgments of state and federal legislatures over many decades.

In a democratic society, the longstanding consensus on the need to limit corporate campaign spending should outweigh the wooden application of judge-made rules. The majority's rejection of this principle "elevate[s] corporations to a level of deference which has not been seen at least since the days when substantive due process was regularly used to invalidate regulatory legislation thought to unfairly impinge upon estab-

---

76. I note that, among the many other regulatory possibilities it has left open, ranging from new versions of § 203 supported by additional evidence of *quid pro quo* corruption or its appearance to any number of tax incentive or public financing schemes, today's decision does not require that a legislature rely solely on these mechanisms to protect shareholders. Legislatures remain free in their incorporation and tax laws to condition the types of activity in which corporations may engage, including electioneering activity, on specific disclosure requirements or on prior express approval by shareholders or members.

lished economic interests." *Bellotti* (White, J., dissenting). At bottom, the Court's opinion is thus a rejection of the common sense of the American people, who have recognized a need to prevent corporations from undermining self-government since the founding, and who have fought against the distinctive corrupting potential of corporate electioneering since the days of Theodore Roosevelt. It is a strange time to repudiate that common sense. While American democracy is imperfect, few outside the majority of this Court would have thought its flaws included a dearth of corporate money in politics.

I would affirm the judgment of the District Court.

[The dissent by JUSTICE THOMAS is omitted. He would have also struck down BCRA's disclosure provisions as unconstitutional.]

NOTES ON CITIZENS UNITED AND ITS AFTERMATH

1. *Regulation of Corporate Political Activity After* Citizens United. *Citizens United* considered only independent expenditures by corporations for electioneering communications; it did not change the longstanding rules requiring corporations to set up PACs to make contributions directly to federal candidates for office and to political parties. Federal law includes a series of limitations on contributions made by corporate PACs, all of which still apply; for example, a PAC can contribute only $5,000 to a federal congressional candidate during an election cycle and only $15,000 to a political party per year. (These were not raised or indexed by BCRA, unlike many other limitations on campaign contributions.) Although 24 states have laws that parallel the federal requirements limiting corporate spending in campaigns, other states have long allowed corporations and unions to make contributions and political expenditures from their general treasury funds. So the legal change ushered in by *Citizens United* varies from state to state, and more change may occur in the future as litigants use the Court's reasoning to attack other regulations on corporate political spending.[e]

Does the Court's rationale in *Citizens United* suggest that these restrictions may face challenge because corporations are treated differently from individuals, who do not need to set up segregated funds to donate money? Will the PAC requirements applied to direct contributions to candidates be characterized as a "ban" on corporate speech, as they were by the majority in *Citizens United* in the context of independent expenditures? The language used in the majority opinion in *Citizens United* and by Chief Justice Roberts' opinion in *WRTL* is noteworthy. The requirement that corporations and unions use segregated funds to make political expenditures—which restricts their ability to engage in political speech—is described as a "ban" on corporate speech that "prevents" corporate officials from presenting their views. The FEC is characterized as a "censor," rather than a regulator. Justice Stevens strongly attacks this language as misleading, and he lists the many avenues for speech still open to corporate interests: not only through the use

---

e. For a description of the effect of *Citizens United* on state campaign laws, see National Association of State Legislatures, *Life After* Citizens United (June 15, 2010), http://www.ncsl.org/default.aspx?tabid=19607.

of PACs, but also through speech outside the corporate form by individuals, through *MCFL*-type organizations, through genuine issue advocacy financed by general treasury funds, and through other types of communications. Which characterization of § 203 is the most accurate? How does the language used by both sides frame their arguments? How will language be deployed in the inevitable future challenge to restrictions on political contributions made to candidates by corporations and unions?

Citizens United is an ideological nonprofit, so political spending relating to candidates and political parties lies at the heart of its mission. In contrast, some—perhaps many—for-profit corporations are not eager to take advantage of the ability to use general treasury funds for independent expenditures. Corporations that are now considering how to react to *Citizens United* are concerned that taking political positions in a public way may cause backlash from their consumers or employees.[f] Traditionally, corporate managers have preferred to spend money on lobbying members of Congress rather than on campaign activity because they have viewed lobbying as a more successful and direct means of influencing policy. There was disagreement among corporations about the *Citizens United* case itself. For example, the American Independent Business Alliance, a nonprofit entity supporting locally owned small businesses and entrepreneurs, supported § 203 of BCRA in an *amicus* brief filed with the Court during consideration of *Citizens United*. Among the arguments made by the Alliance was the concern that large corporations would take advantage of the ability to spend directly from their general treasury funds to influence the legislative process in ways that would systematically disadvantage small businesses without the resources to gain access to lawmakers. It noted in particular a concern that such influence would be used to "extract subsidies from taxpayers, stifle enforcement of anti-trust laws, [and] create legal tax evasion opportunities."

Which corporations do you expect will take advantage of the more liberal rules governing independent expenditures? Is their spending likely to help incumbents or challengers more? PAC spending at the federal level has tended to be disproportionately targeted to incumbent members of Congress, regardless of political affiliation. With corporations now able to spend significantly more money on independent political expenditures, will businesses face pressure from legislators to play more active roles in federal campaigns? In an analysis of the corruption rationale in campaign finance cases published well before *Citizens United*, Professor David Strauss identified an element of extortion in a system "in which campaign contributions are freely exchanged for official action." Under these conditions, "there is a danger that representatives may coerce potential contributors, in effect extorting contributions by the threat that they will act against the contributor's interests." *Corruption, Equality, and Campaign Finance Reform*, 94 Colum. L. Rev. 1369, 1380 (1994). This notion is related to the idea of rent extraction discussed in the casebook at pp. 61–62. Are particular industries more likely to be the target of this manipulation by lawmakers seeking reelection? Is the possibility of such "extortion" reduced because *Citizens United* applies only to independent expenditures by corporations and unions, or can pressure still be applied? Is

---

f. See Carol Leonnig, *Political ads are a tough sell for image-conscious corporations*, Wash. Post, June 1, 2010.

this kind of corruption likely to persuade the Supreme Court to uphold some restrictions on corporate political spending?

What other changes in the landscape of federal campaigns do you expect after *Citizens United*? Justice Stevens provided one prediction in his dissent: "By removing one of its central components, today's ruling makes a hash out of BCRA's 'delicate and interconnected regulatory scheme.' *McConnell*. Consider just one example of the distortions that will follow: Political parties are barred under BCRA from soliciting or spending 'soft money,' funds that are not subject to the statute's disclosure requirements or its source and amount limitations. Going forward, corporations and unions will be free to spend as much general treasury money as they wish on ads that support or attack specific candidates, whereas national parties will not be able to spend a dime of soft money on ads of any kind. The Court's ruling thus dramatically enhances the role of corporations and unions—and the narrow interests they represent—vis-à-vis the role of political parties—and the broad coalitions they represent—in determining who will hold public office." *Citizens United*, 130 S.Ct. at 940 (Stevens, J. concurring in part and dissenting in part). Professor Nathaniel Persily agreed that "political parties as institutions were probably losers," but then wondered whether that would improve campaigns or affect them negatively. "[T]he extreme cohesiveness and polarization of the political parties might be countered by independent, non-party bases of support that influence candidates. At the same time (and more likely from my view), the decision might polarize the parties even further, because independent spenders tend to come from and support extreme positions."[g] Of course, after BCRA was passed, drastically limiting soft money contributions to political parties, many predicted that parties would be significantly weakened while 527 organizations and other groups often focused on only one issue would disproportionately influence federal elections. Although 527 organizations have played a larger role in campaigns since BCRA, political parties have remained key players.

2. *The Corruption Interest after* Citizens United. The idea of *quid pro quo* corruption has evolved since *Buckley*, as the Court has worked to define what constitutes this sort of corruption, in actuality and appearance. The Court clearly rejected *Austin*'s articulation of political corruption, which it called the "antidistortion interest." But the opinion contains language that may be used in the future to limit or reshape the understanding of the more traditional *quid pro quo* corruption deemed sufficient to justify regulation. Remember that *McConnell* had expanded *quid pro quo* corruption to encompass the "special access" that larger donors obtain, or that ordinary voters worry they might have obtained. Justice Kennedy, the author of the majority in *Citizens United*, took issue with this formulation in his separate opinion in *McConnell*, arguing that access is part of the democratic process. (Casebook, pp. 286–87.) Perhaps not surprisingly then, Justice Kennedy cited his *McConnell* opinion on this issue at length in *Citizens United*, and noted that "[t]he fact that speakers may have influence over or access to elected officials does not mean that these officials are corrupt." 130 S.Ct. at 910. Furthermore, the majority opinion seems to limit the reach of the appearance of corruption

---

g. Nathaniel Persily, Citizens United: *Qui Bono and Que Sera*, Balkinization blog (Jan. 25, 2010), http://balkin.blogspot.com/2010/01/citizens-united-qui-bono-and-que-sera.html.

rationale: "The appearance of influence or access * * * will not cause the electorate to lose faith in our democracy. * * * In fact, there is only scant evidence that independent expenditures even ingratiate. * * * Ingratiation and access, in any event, are not corruption." *Id.* at 910–11.

Justice Kennedy also questioned the evidence in *McConnell* that the Court then had found sufficient to uphold the regulation. Although the record in that case was more than 100,000 pages long, the *Citizens United* majority observed that there were no direct examples of votes being exchanged for political expenditures. Considered together with the language disparaging special access as an indication of corruption that might undermine the integrity of democratic institutions, this discussion seems to increase the quantum and change the character of evidence required to provide a foundation for regulation. How realistic is it to expect lawmakers to produce a record with specific examples of votes changed on account of financial support in campaigns? Wasn't that difficulty the reason that *Buckley* included the "appearance" of such corruption that exists when the political system allows large contributions from wealthy interests, rather than limiting the state interest to one supported by proof of actual corruption? Does the *Citizens United* majority reduce the governmental interest of *quid pro quo* corruption back to the bribery-like behavior, and move away from the expansion of that concept that the Court had developed in *Shrink Missouri PAC* (casebook, p. 243) and *McConnell*?

3. *Developments Affecting Section 527 Organizations.* The influence of Section 527 groups in the 2004 campaign (casebook, pp. 288–90), led to a regulatory response by the Federal Election Commission effective January 2005. Generally, the regulation sought to require that nonprofit groups that register as political committees—those that take in or spend more than $1,000 a year to influence federal elections and that have a "major purpose" relating to federal elections—use more "hard money" for various political activities, rather than "soft money." (Remember that hard money is subject to federal regulation, including campaign contribution limitations, and soft money is largely unregulated, except for some disclosure.) So, for example, the FEC required that these organizations use only hard money for any communication relating to a federal candidate, and pay for at least 50% of the cost of get-out-the-vote efforts for political parties with hard money.

EMILY's List, a nonprofit 527 organization that supports pro-choice Democratic women candidates, sued, arguing the regulation violated the First Amendment; the D.C. Court of Appeals agreed and vacated the regulation. *EMILY's List v. Federal Election Comm'n*, 581 F.3d 1 (D.C. Cir. 2009). It characterized EMILY's List as a hybrid political committee: one that makes contributions to candidates directly (which clearly can be regulated through, among other things, contribution limitations) and that makes political expenditures itself for get-out-the-vote efforts and political advertisements (which cannot be regulated as heavily, particularly after *Citizens United*, which was handed down after this case). The appellate court held: "A non-profit that makes expenditures to support federal candidates does not suddenly forfeit its First Amendment rights when it decides also to make direct contributions to parties or candidates. Rather, it simply must ensure, to avoid circumvention of individual contribution limits by its donors, that its contributions to parties or candidates come from a hard-money account." *Id.* at 12. It therefore struck down the FEC's regulation of 527 organizations because it aimed to regulate independent political expenditures by organizations like EMILY's List.

The court distinguished political parties, which no longer have much access to soft money in federal campaigns because of BCRA's provisions, and nonprofit political groups because "there is no record evidence that non-profit entities have sold access to federal candidates and officeholders in exchange for large contributions." *Id.* at 14. Thus, the FEC erred when it attempted to use its regulatory power to apply similar soft money restrictions to nonprofits as Congress had applied to parties. Because the decision is based on constitutional grounds, however, it seems to foreclose legislative changes that would restrict Section 527 organizations' use of soft money.[h] When this decision is combined with *Citizens United*, does it reinforce Justice Stevens' prediction that parties will become significantly less influential than corporations, non-profit and for-profit, that wish to be politically engaged?

After *Citizens United*, the D.C. Circuit handed down a second important case affecting 527 organizations; this decision further increased the ability of these nonprofit organizations to influence federal campaigns. In *Speech-Now.org v. Federal Election Comm'n*, 599 F.3d 686 (D.C. Cir. 2010) (en banc), the appellate court prohibited the FEC from requiring SpeechNow.org to register as a PAC, thereby subjecting it to contribution limitations. Speech-Now.org is an unincorporated nonprofit organization that promotes its view of the First Amendment in a variety of ways, including through advertisements supporting federal candidates who share its views and opposing those it believes are not sufficiently committed to the First Amendment. Donors wanted to contribute more than $5,000 (the limit on contributions to PACs) to the nonprofit so that SpeechNow.org could produce ads attacking two incumbent lawmakers in the 2010 election cycle. In this as-applied challenge decided using the framework of *Citizens United*, Judge Sentelle's unanimous opinion found no acceptable state interest to justify limiting contributions to this ideological nonprofit that was only making independent expenditures in federal campaigns. He wrote: "[B]ecause *Citizens United* holds that independent expenditures do not corrupt or give the appearance of corruption as a matter of law, then the government can have no anti-corruption interest in limiting contributions to independent expenditure-only organizations." *Id.* at 696. Consistent with *Citizens United*, the court allowed application of disclosure requirements and other administrative regulations to this organization. The combination of these rulings means that independent-expenditure-only 527 organizations are free both of limitations on contributions to them and of restrictions on their independent campaign expenditures advocating for the victory or defeat of federal candidates.

Section 527 organization remain active in federal campaigns, but not at the levels they reached in 2004. Section 527s spent $200 million in 2008, less than half of the amount that Section 527s spent in the 2004 election cycle.[i]

---

h. The concurrence argued that the regulations should have been vacated because the FEC lacked the statutory authority to promulgate them and leave the constitutional issues for another day. See *EMILY's List*, 581 F.3d at 25–26 (Brown, concurring).

i. Campaign Finance Institute, *Soft Money Political Spending by 501(c) Nonprofits Tripled in 2008 Election* (Feb. 2009), http://www.cfinst.org/Press/PReleases/09–02–25/Soft_Money_Political_Spending_by_Nonprofits_Tripled_in_2008.aspx.

Increasingly, political groups are using other nonprofit structures, such as 501(c)(4) organizations—which are civic and social welfare organizations that promote the "common good and general welfare" and that can engage in political activity that is issue driven. Citizens United is a nonprofit organized under Section 501(c)(4). One advantage of the 501(c)(4) structure is that, unlike Section 527 groups, there is no legal requirement for them to disclose their individual donors. It is estimated that 501(c)(4) groups may have spent more than $200 million in federal elections in 2008,[j] and that figure may increase given the more permissive regulatory structure ushered in by *Citizens United*. The organization of political groups can be stunningly complex, as one group may use various nonprofit structures—including, to a limited extent, charitable 501(c)(3) organizations—to arrange its political activities to provide the most flexibility, sometimes the most protection against disclosure, and the greatest ability to raise funds.

4. *Immediate Legislative Response to* Citizens United. Political reactions to the Court's decision were swift and varied. Republican Senate Leader Mitch McConnell (Ky.), the lead plaintiff in the *McConnell* case, said the ruling "struck a blow for the First Amendment." John McCain (R–Ariz.) released a surprisingly restrained statement, considering that he coauthored BCRA and portrays himself as a reform maverick, merely saying he was "disappointed" by the decision. A tough reelection battle in a conservative state may explain his muted response. Other lawmakers attacked the ruling in *Citizens United* as unleashing the possibility that wealthy, for-profit corporations would distort the political process and dominate the public debate surrounding federal candidate elections. The Chairman of the Senate Judiciary Committee, Patrick Leahy (D–Vt.), criticized the opinion on the Senate floor, saying the ruling "goes to the very core of our democracy, and it will allow major corporations—who should have laws written to control their effect on America—instead control America."

The most memorable attack occurred days after the decision came out, when President Obama criticized the ruling in his State of the Union address, which most Supreme Court Justices attended. "With all due deference to separation of powers," he said, the Court "reversed a century of law that I believe will open the floodgates for special interests—including foreign corporations—to spend without limit in our elections." Although the Justices typically sit impassively through the speech, Justice Alito was caught by the cameras reacting angrily to the President's charge.

Federal lawmakers, as well as legislators in states with laws brought into question by *Citizens United*, pondered possible legislative responses that could survive court challenge. Some reform proposals centered on corporate law. For example, the Brennan Center for Justice proposed a Shareholder's Rights Act to require that shareholders vote at a public corporation's annual meeting to authorize the use of general treasury funds for political expenditures.[k] It

---

j. See Erika Lunder & Paige Whitaker, Congressional Research Service, *501(c)(4) Organizations and Campaign Activity: Analysis Under Tax and Campaign Finance Laws* 1 (Jan. 29, 2009) (citing Campaign Finance Institute estimates).

k. Ciara Torres–Spelliscy, *Corporate Campaign Spending: Giving Shareholders a Voice* 25–26 (2010).

would amend the Securities Exchange Act of 1934 to require periodic public disclosure of corporate political activities. If a public corporation makes political expenditures without first obtaining shareholder approval, then the directors would be forced to repay the corporation, with interest. Several states began to consider similar changes in their corporate law codes.

Other reforms were inspired by the Court's strong affirmation of disclosure provisions. Democrats in the Senate and the House introduced The DISCLOSE Act (The Democracy is Strengthened by Casting Light on Spending in Elections Act). The Act proposes enhanced disclosure provisions for nonprofit and for-profit corporations, as well as unions. These include requirements that a CEO or organization leader appear at the end of the broadcast advertisement to affirm that she "approves this message," that the top five contributors to the organization be listed on the screen, and that groups inform their shareholders and members about political spending. It would also ban spending by corporations with substantial foreign ownership or control, and political spending by government contractors and recipients of federal bailout funds for financial institutions (TARP). Are any of these provisions constitutionally problematic? What state interests justify the proposed regulations?

The DISCLOSE Act faced significant opposition when it reached the floor of the House—opposition that extended beyond the expected disapproval of most Republicans. First, conservative Democrats were concerned about the opposition of groups like the U.S. Chamber of Commerce, the National Federation of Independent Business, and the National Association of Realtors. Most importantly, however, some Democrats, facing reelection battles in the fall in conservative states, demanded that congressional leadership and the White House agree to exempt the National Rifle Association from the bill's coverage.[1] A exemption was drafted that applied to organizations with more than one million members, with members in all 50 states, in existence for more than 10 years, and that raised 15% or less of their funds from corporations. When it turned out that only the NRA met these requirements, the exemption was amended to cover organizations with more than 500,000 members, thereby also exempting the Sierra Club, the Humane Society, and the American Association of Retired Persons. Not only did this exemption call into question the constitutionality of the bill because it is difficult to construct a justification for treating these organizations differently from all others seeking to exercise their First Amendment rights (other than sheer political power), but it also provoked a backlash from liberal Democrats. Groups like the Congressional Black Caucus became concerned that progressive organizations they supported would be disadvantaged relative to the lucky few that fell within the scope of the exemption. The bill, containing the exemption, managed to pass the House by a vote of 219 to 206 in June 2010, but substantial opposition was expected in the Senate, where a filibuster could slow down or derail the reform. Chances for enactment in time for the 2010 elections seemed slim.

---

1. For a description of this legislative saga, see Kenneth Vogel, Jonathan Allen, & John Bresnahan, *How Dems' NRA Loophole Backfired*, Politico.com (June 18, 2010), http://www.politico.com/news/stories/0610/38713.html.

C. STATE REFORMS AND PUBLIC FINANCING

Page 295. Add after the citation in the first paragraph to *Nixon v. Shrink Missouri PAC*:

(In 2008, Missouri's legislature repealed state limits on contributions, while requiring disclosure of contributions of $5,000 or more within 48 hours.)

Page 297. Add the following footnote p to the third sentence of the paragraph:

p. Arizona's public financing system was upheld against a First Amendment attack in May 2010. *McComish v. Bennett*, 605 F.3d 720 (9th Cir. 2010), *stay granted,* 78 U.S.L.W. 3728 (June 8, 2010). The Court distinguished the case from *FEC v. Davis* (supplement, p. 13), in which the Supreme Court struck down BCRA's "millionaire opponent" provision, because the state's Clean Elections law allowed candidates to opt-in to public financing and did not allocate money or benefits specifically to opponents of wealthy candidates. Indeed, *Buckley* had upheld the presidential system of public funding, and no other Supreme Court precedent has drawn that conclusion into question. The state regulatory system served *Buckley*'s anticorruption rationale because candidates receiving public money "relinquish their right to raise campaign contributions from private donors. They therefore have both reduced opportunities and reduced incentives to trade legislative favors for financial favors." The decision of the U.S. Supreme Court to stay the mandate of the Ninth Circuit's decision and allow the District Court's injunction of the act to remain in effect signaled that it is likely the Justices will grant the petition for certiorari and hear the case.

CHAPTER 3

STRUCTURES OF LEGISLATIVE DELIBERATION

■ ■ ■

SECTION 1. REGULATING "CORRUPT" DELIBERATION

C. CONFLICTS OF INTEREST

Page 313. Add the following before 2. *Outside earned income is limited:*

A recent Oregon Supreme Court case dealt with a First Amendment challenge to that state's gift restrictions. *Vannatta v. Oregon Government Ethics Commission*, 222 P.3d 1077 (Ore. 2009). A registered lobbyist attacked the gift ban and the restriction on the offering of gifts to lawmakers as an unconstitutional burden on expression protected by the First Amendment. The plaintiff argued that the law, by prohibiting gifts to lawmakers that exceeded $50 in value in a calendar year, banned "expenditures designed to facilitate dialogue and obtain goodwill with public officials." He also contended that the restrictions on communicating offers of gifts discriminated among speech on the basis of conduct and interfered with the constitutionally protected right to petition government for redress of grievances. The court rejected the attack on the provisions dealing with receipt of gifts because this action is not expressive conduct, and lawmakers and citizens, including lobbyists, can communicate and engage in the range of official conduct without also providing gifts to the public officials. It ruled, however, that the ban on offering gifts above the threshold did impermissibly burden speech and noted that the restrictions on offering gifts were not intended to curtail invidious behavior but were focused on the mere "utterance of an offer" without regard to its effects on behavior. *Id.* at 1086. Are the federal gift restrictions subject to similar First Amendment attack, either as political expression or as an intrinsic part of petitioning the government for policy change?

SECTION 2. LOBBYING

B. THE FEDERAL LOBBYING DISCLOSURE ACT: STRENGTHENING AND EXPANDING DISCLOSURE REQUIREMENTS

Page 344. Add the following at the end of the second line:

The Center for Responsive Politics reported that spending on federal lobbying in 2009 exceeded $3.49 billion. During that year, the top industries with regard to lobbying expenses were pharmaceutical businesses ($267 million), business associations ($183 million), oil and gas ($174 million), the insurance industry ($164 million), electric utilities (nearly $145 million), and computer makers and the Internet industry ($119 million). The Chamber of Commerce (and its affiliates) again led with respect to individual companies and trade organizations that are active in Washington, shelling out more than $144 million on in-house lobbyists and hired firms in 2009. The second highest spender, ExxonMobil, was dwarfed by the Chamber of Commerce, only spending $27 million. The Chamber of Commerce increased spending between 2007 and 2009 by more than 250%.[a]

Page 347. Add the following before Lobbying Disclosure Act Problems:

The first challenge to the Lobbying Disclosure Act was brought in 2008 after HLOGA changed the rules affecting disclosure of members of a coalition that is engaged in lobbying. The provision at issue was Section 4(b)(3), on page 339 of the casebook; it requires any registrant under the LDA to provide information about any organization that contributes more than $5,000 to fund its lobbying activities and that "actively participates" in the "planning, supervision, or control" of the activities. The statute seeks to protect individuals who are members of such an organization from disclosure (casebook, p. 339), instead targeting only organizations. The National Association of Manufacturers (NAM), the country's largest trade organization with more than 11,000 corporate members, challenged this provision under the First Amendment. NAM argued that disclosure of its members would chill them from participating in the political process for fear of the consequences of such publicity. It also contended that the provisions were unconstitutionally vague.

The appellate court unanimously sustained the law against the attack in *National Association of Manufacturers v. Taylor*, 582 F.3d 1 (D.C. Cir. 2009). In applying a strict scrutiny standard, the court identified the compelling state interest behind the disclosure statute as revealing to the public the interests behind coalitions of organizations, including, but not limited to, so-called "stealth coalitions." It relied on the long line of cases affirming disclosure statutes in a variety of political contexts—lobbying and campaign finance regulation—to demonstrate the legitimacy of the congressional objective of providing information to the public about the effect of paid lobbying on

---

a. See Center for Responsive Politics, *Lobbying Database* (Apr. 25, 2010), http://www.open secrets.org/lobby/index.php.

federal policy. It held that the provision was appropriately tailored to vindicate the state's interest in transparency. The court also found the LDA was not impermissibly vague; for example, other laws that did even more than require disclosure of political activity using a standard like "actively participates" have been upheld. See, e.g., *U.S. Civil Service Commission v. National Association of Letter Carriers*, 413 U.S. 548 (1973) (rejecting a similar attack on the Hatch Act, which bars federal employees from taking "an active part" in managing political campaigns). Moreover, the LDA has been in effect since 1995 with no reported problems of registrants not understanding what constituted "lobbying activities."

The court also considered NAM's argument that, even if the provision is facially constitutional, it was nonetheless problematic as applied to NAM's members. The organization had provided examples of some of the consequences its members feared from disclosure: "[M]ob violence has been directed at firms targeted by anti-globalization forces. * * * Firms that are identified as actively lobbying on issues relating to on-going litigation, e.g., asbestos, risk becoming litigation targets. Taking policy positions that are unpopular with some groups may lead to boycotts, shareholder suits, demands for political contributions or support, and other forms of harassment." There was, however, no evidence of the kind of serious harm or retaliation suffered by the members of the Socialist Workers Party or the NAACP that had led courts to exempt those organizations from disclosing their members (casebook, pp. 346–47). Indeed, the court noted that NAM's website already identified more than 250 members, none of which produced evidence of adverse consequences from that publicity.

NOTE ON OBAMA ADMINISTRATION RULES CONCERNING LOBBYISTS

The Obama Administration took a very hard line with respect to the ability of registered lobbyists to work in the administration and imposed significant post-employment restrictions on officials. On his first day in office, the President issued an executive order laying out an ethics pledge required of all executive branch appointees. Exec. Order No. 13490, 74 Fed. Reg. 4673 (Jan. 26, 2009). The teeth of the pledge is a provision that bans any appointed official who is a registered lobbyist from participating in any matter on which she lobbied within the last two years or "in any specific issue areas in which that particular matter falls." In other words, someone who was a registered lobbyist for an environmental group advocating for a green energy bill could not work on policy relating to energy issues, climate change proposals, or environmental policy relating to energy. This has essentially kept lobbyists out of the executive branch—not just lobbyists from corporate America, but also people involved in nonprofits who registered as lobbyists because of their contacts with legislative and executive branch officials on their policy reform issues. Waivers have been allowed in a few instances, including for a former Raytheon lobbyist to become Deputy Secretary of Defense and a former lobbyist for Goldman Sachs to become the Secretary of Treasury's Chief of Staff. The bad press surrounding these exceptions soon convinced the administration to grant even fewer, including with respect to people who came from the reform sector.

In addition, the ethics pledge requires that a registered lobbyist cannot seek employment with any executive branch agency that she lobbied in the past two years. Finally, the ethics pledge also contains a provision aiming broadly at the "revolving door" between government and lobbying. It restricts outgoing appointees from lobbying any covered executive branch official anywhere in the federal government during the entirety of the Obama Administration's tenure in office.

In addition to this broad restriction on lobbyists, President Obama also imposed strict limitations on lobbying activity with regard to the expenditure of money provided by the American Recovery and Reinvestment Act of 2009 (the economic stimulus bill).[b] Registered lobbyists are prohibited from making oral communications to executive branch officials about particular projects or applications under the stimulus act (other than general questions about logistics), and all written communications must be posted by agencies on a public website. The President justified these restrictions with the argument that "[w]e must not allow Recovery Act funds to be distributed on the basis of factors other than the merits of proposed projects or in response to improper influence or pressure." Finally, the Obama Administration announced that it plans to reduce the number of registered lobbyists serving on the nearly 1,000 federal advisory panels, which have more than 60,000 members. The White House Ethics Adviser defended this position because lobbyists "traffic in relationships, working both the Congress and federal agencies to bend legislation and policies on behalf of their clients."[c]

One effect of the Obama rules, as well as of the anti-lobbyist rhetoric that characterized his campaign and continued into the President's term of office, has been a demand for formal methods of de-registering as a lobbyist. Before the new rules, some would register even when they might not clearly meet the requirements or would continue to be registered because there was no perceived disadvantage to registration and disclosure. Instead, people were counseled to register and remain registered when in doubt—better safe than sorry. As soon as the status of lobbyist resulted in concrete negative consequences, however, the Secretary of the Senate and the Clerk of the House— the officials responsible for the registration system—began to receive questions about de-registering. In June 2009, they released guidance about terminating registrations if a currently registered lobbyist "reasonably" expects that she will not be making lobbying contacts on behalf of a client at any time in the future, or if she spent less than 20% of her time lobbying over the current or upcoming six-month period.[d] The guidance does not allow retroactive de-registering, something some lobbyists had sought so that they could qualify to serve in the Obama Administration. In the second quarter of 2009, 1,418 lobbyists de-registered, and the number of lobbyists de-registering since the beginning of 2008 has outpaced the number of new registrations.[e] Anecdo-

---

b. President Barack Obama, *Memorandum of March 20, 2009: Ensuring Responsible Spending of Recovery Act Funds*, 74 Fed. Reg. 12531 (Mar. 25, 2009).

c. Anna Palmer, *Lobby League Pressures White House on Advisory Boards*, Roll Call, Oct. 28, 2009.

d. See Lobbying Disclosure Act Guidance (revised June 2010), http://lobbyingdisclosure.house.gov/amended_lda_guide.html#section8.

e. See Dave Levinthal, *Lobbyists Terminating Their Federal Registrations at Accelerated Rate* (Nov. 2 2009), http://www.opensecrets.org/news/2009/11/lobbyists-terminating-their-fe.html.

tally, some observers note that many who might have been willing to register as lobbyists before President Obama was elected have avoided that process and portray themselves as "senior advisors" on policy, giving rise to fears that the administration's policies may have actually reduced transparency. The number of lobbyists registered federally declined to 11,014 in September 2009, down from a peak of 13,428 in mid–2007.

SECTION 3.   RULES FACILITATING LEGISLATIVE DELIBERATION

B.   THE LINE ITEM VETO: A RULE TO ENFORCE BUDGET LIMITATIONS

Page 371. Add the following at the end of the third line:

Another referendum was passed by Wisconsin voters in 2008 to further limit the Governor's line item veto, which had become known as the "Frankenstein veto" because he could still, through strategic editing, stitch two sentences together to form a new sentence with a different meaning. The new law prohibits the Governor from creating "a new sentence by combining parts of two or more sentences," but still allows the Governor the power to veto parts of appropriations bills and other provisions that are considered "items." See Wis. Const. Art. V, § 10(c) (2010).

CHAPTER 4

DUE PROCESS OF LAWMAKING

■ ■ ■

SECTION 1. STRUCTURAL DUE PROCESS

A. CONSTITUTIONAL REQUIREMENTS FOR THE PROCEDURES FOLLOWED IN STATE AND FEDERAL LAWMAKING

Page 415. Add after *Problem 4–1* the following new problem:

Problem 4–1a: Much like the Civil Rights Act story that began the casebook (pp. 2–23), supporters of the Patient Protection and Affordable Care Act (PPACA)—the comprehensive health reform act that passed in Spring 2010—knew the bill could not survive a conference committee. The House of Representatives had passed one version of the bill in late 2009; the Senate passed a different version on Christmas Eve 2009, managing to get 60 votes to overcome a filibuster. Reconciling the two bills appeared a daunting task, particularly after Republican Scott Brown was elected to the seat long occupied by the late Senator Edward M. Kennedy (D–Mass.), undermining the fragile consensus that had allowed supermajority support. The House demanded changes to the bill, and the President and party leaders decided to adopt those changes through a budget reconciliation vehicle that can be passed by a simple majority in the Senate (casebook, p. 461). A pivotal group of House Democrats wanted to enact both bills at the same time, and they preferred to record their votes only on the package of amendments without going on record in support of the Senate version. There were also concerns that if the House enacted the Senate's version of PPACA first and then waited to pass the reconciliation law with the "fixes," the second bill would not make it through the congressional labyrinth.

Some proposed a solution: a procedure called "deem and pass" that had been used in other, less salient situations. Under the deem and pass process, a House rule governing the reconciliation bill would provide that when the House voted on and passed the legislation, it would also be deemed to have passed the Senate's version of PPACA at the same time. However, no separate vote on the Senate bill would ever occur in the House; rather, by a single vote, both bills would pass. In the end, the deem and pass solution was not used, and both bills—the Senate's version of health care and the reconciliation package enacting amendments to it—were enacted. Deem and pass was discarded as an option in part because lawmakers became concerned that the health care reform bill would be subject to constitutional attack that it had not been "passed" or "approved" by the House. One response to this claim was that the enrolled bill rule would ensure that a court would not look past a properly enrolled bill to analyze the process through which one house adopted it. Which argument is persuasive? Does the deem and pass technique raise other constitutional issues?[a]

SECTION 2.   THE FEDERAL CONGRESSIONAL BUDGET PROCESS

B.   THE BUDGET ENFORCEMENT ACT OF 1990 AND THE POLITICS OF OFFSETS

Pages 466–67. Delete the last two sentences of the paragraph that runs from the bottom of page 466 to the top of page 467, and insert the following:

Any optimism about the federal budget disappeared in 2007 when the country suffered the gravest economic downturn since the Great Depression. The Bush Administration and then the new Obama Administration responded with a series of initiatives to shore up the financial industry, bail out domestic automobile companies, increase support for unemployed Americans, and stimulate the economy through federal spending and tax breaks. In January 2010, the Congressional Budget Office projected a deficit of $1.3 trillion for fiscal year 2010, the second largest since World War II (as a share of the GDP). *The Budget and Economic Outlook: Fiscal Year 2010 to 2020* (Jan. 2010). Total debt was expected to reach $8.8 trillion by the end of 2010, which is 60 percent of GDP and the highest level since the 1950s. The dire economic conditions underscored the dilemma politicians faced as they considered whether to let the tax cuts enacted during the Bush years expire at the end of 2010, and thereby effectively increase taxes on all Americans at a time of economic distress. The CBO report noted that if all the tax provisions scheduled to expire were extended, deficits over the next decade would be $7 trillion higher. Although it seems likely that tax cuts enjoyed by Americans with higher incomes will expire, Democrats and Republicans alike hope to retain the lower tax rates for lower- and middle-income taxpayers.

A major factor in the growth of the deficit is the burgeoning cost of entitlement programs, particularly the health entitlements like Medicare and Medicaid. President Obama has argued that the comprehensive health care legislation enacted in 2010 will ultimately reduce the federal deficit by controlling health care costs, but that conclusion is controversial, and many believe that costs will increase in the near term, with any savings

---

a. Compare Michael McConnell, *The House Health–Care Vote and the Constitution*, Wall St. J., Mar. 15, 2010, and *The Health Vote and the Constitution–II*, Wall St. J., Mar. 19, 2010, with Vikram Amar, *A Bill's Text, its Whole Text and Nothing But its Text? The Flap Over "Deem and Pass" in the Health Care Debate, and a Look at How a Bill Becomes a Law*, Findlaw, Mar. 26, 2010, *available at* http://writ.news.findlaw.com/amar/20100326.html.

coming later, if at all. Given the economic situation, the temporary nature of a large part of the tax code, and the adoption of new federal programs, the country's fiscal situation is at best very uncertain and at worst completely unsustainable.

Page 468. Add at the end of the first paragraph:

Congress enacted new PAYGO legislation early in 2010, putting it back into statutory form for the first time since 2002. Just as with earlier versions of statutory PAYGO, the process applies only to proposed legislation that affects tax revenues and direct spending programs, and it requires "budget neutrality" over five- and ten-year windows. It explicitly exempts from its reach several pending (and potentially costly) proposals, including the extension of expiring tax cuts for middle-income Americans and changes in the alternative minimum tax and estate tax that were expected to be considered in subsequent months.[b]

Pages 468–69. Delete the last two sentences in the paragraph that runs from the bottom of page 468 to the top of page 469, and replace with the following:

When Congress again adopted PAYGO in statutory form in 2010, it included enforcement through sequestration implemented by the executive branch—that is, across-the-board cuts in nonexempt direct spending programs (although, as in the past, many entitlement programs are exempt from the threat of sequestration).

Page 485. Add at the end of *Problem 4–7*:

(In March 2010, the House Appropriations Committee banned all earmarks relating to for-profit entities; in response, the House Republicans adopted a one-year moratorium on all earmarks proposed by their members. The durability of these agreements is not certain.)

SECTION 3.   OTHER CONGRESSIONAL STRUCTURES

Page 513. Replace the last full sentence on the page with the following:

In the 109th Congress, the Senate required 60 votes to waive an UMRA point of order, but in the following Congress, when the Democrats regained control, the Senate returned to the rule that a majority vote is sufficient to dispense with the objection.[c]

---

b. Robert Keith, Congressional Research Service, *The Statutory Pay–As–You–Go Act of 2010: Summary and Legislative History* 8–12 (Apr. 2, 2010).

c. Elizabeth Garrett, *Framework Legislation and Federalism*, 83 Notre Dame L. Rev. 1495, 1502 (2008).

CHAPTER 5

DIRECT DEMOCRACY

■ ■ ■

SECTION 1. AN OVERVIEW OF DIRECT DEMOCRACY

Page 532. Add the following at the end of footnote c:

For a discussion of the First Amendment implications of subject matter restrictions and relevant judicial decisions, see Anna Skiba–Crafts, *Note: Conditions on Taking the Initiative: The First Amendment Implications of Subject Matter Restrictions on Ballot Initiatives*, 107 Mich. L. Rev. 1305 (2009).

Page 533. Add the following before "Effect on the Lawmaking Agenda":

*NOTE ON THE INTERNET AND ATTACKS ON DISCLOSURE
RELATING TO BALLOT MEASURES*

Generally, disclosure statutes in both candidate and ballot measure elections have been upheld by courts as constitutionally permissible under the First Amendment. For example, in *First National Bank of Boston v. Bellotti*, 435 U.S. 765 (1978), in which the Supreme Court struck down prohibitions on corporate expenditures in issue campaigns, the Court also noted "[i]dentification of the source of advertising may be required as a means of disclosure, so that people will be able to evaluate the arguments to which they are being subjected." *Id.* at 792 n.32. Similarly, when the Court struck down contribution limits in direct democracy, it observed that "[t]he integrity of the political system will be adequately protected if contributors are identified in a public filing revealing the amounts contributed; if it is thought wise, legislation can outlaw anonymous contributions." *Citizens Against Rent Control v. City of Berkeley*, 454 U.S. 290, 299–300 (1981). Disclosure statutes sometimes have gone too far to meet the Court's "exacting scrutiny," such as the Ohio disclosure law that was applied to Mrs. McIntyre, who was disseminating anonymous leaflets in a campaign concerning a school board referendum. *McIntyre v. Ohio Elections Commission*, 514 U.S. 334 (1995). But *McIntyre* was concerned about ordinary citizens engaging in small-scale political speech; it has not generally been extended to laws requiring that information about political expenditures be reported to a government agency.

50

The growth of the Internet—together with the ease with which people can access information disclosed to state agencies and made available on public websites—may have changed the balance under the First Amendment, particularly when it comes to disclosure of the identity of people making relatively small contributions to a committee involved in an initiative or referendum campaign. The issues have been raised clearly in two recent cases. The first grows out of Proposition 8 in California, the ballot measure that amended the state constitution to deny marriage to same-sex couples. After opponents of same-sex marriage won in a tight contest, supporters of same-sex marriage created a website, Eightmaps.com, that provided the names of the donors to the winning side, their addresses, the amount they contributed, and their occupations. The format through which the information was conveyed—a "mash-up" of Google maps and the Prop 8 donor data posted by the Secretary of State—enables people to easily check whether their neighbors, co-workers, and acquaintances had supported the controversial ballot measure. Gay rights activists provided lists of contributors in other venues as well, including Facebook, Craigslist, and other social networking sites. They urged people who supported same-sex marriage to boycott businesses owned or run by those contributors, and there were allegations of threatening emails and phone calls.[a]

After the election, several ballot committees that had been formed to support the passage of Proposition 8, and thereby to end same-sex marriage, sought an exemption from the state's disclosure provisions. *ProtectMarriage.com v. Bowen*, 599 F. Supp. 2d 1197 (E.D. Cal. 2009) (denying plaintiffs' request for a preliminary injunction). They alleged that, because personal information about donors is available on the Secretary of State's website, Prop 8 supporters and their businesses had been subject to threats, reprisals, and harassment. Among other allegations, they claimed that Fresno Mayor Alan Autry and Pastor Jim Franklin, both Proposition 8 supporters, had received death threats. The plaintiffs also claimed that some supporters had been forced to resign from their jobs; others had property vandalized. Their arguments focused in particular on the $100 threshold for disclosure. ProtectMarriage.com contended that the state had no compelling interest in revealing personal information about individuals whose contributions were so small.

The District Court denied the request for a preliminary injunction, but the trial on the merits continues, with discovery underway. The judge did not view the contributors to Proposition 8 as facing the same threats that the Socialist Workers Party demonstrated with respect to its members in the case that exempted it from federal campaign disclosure laws. See *Brown v. Socialist Workers '74 Campaign Comm. (Ohio)*, 459 U.S. 87 (1982). The 60 members of the Socialist Workers Party experienced destruction of their property, hate mail and threatening phone calls, harassment by the police, and the firing of shots into the Party's offices. In contrast, the donors to Proposition 8 are not part of a "fringe organization" out of step with the views of the majority. On the contrary, they were able to win in a statewide election, receiving more than seven million votes supporting their position. They did not face government persecution or widespread vilification; rather, they "sought to legislate a

---

a. See David Lourie, *Note: Rethinking Donor Disclosure After the Proposition 8 Campaign*, 83 S. Cal. L. Rev. 133 (2009).

concept steeped in tradition and history." *ProtectMarriage.com*, 599 F. Supp. 2d at 1215. While decrying any illegal actions taken against Prop 8 supporters, the court also noted that the First Amendment allows dissent through speech, debate, and even economic boycotts.

Perhaps the most difficult issue posed by this case is whether the state interest justifying disclosure of contributors in a ballot measure campaign— the interest in providing important information to voters—is really implicated with regard to donations of $100 or so by individuals. The judge in *Protect-Marriage.com* described this informational interest in the language of voting cues (casebook, pp. 531–33): Voters "often base their decisions to vote for or against [a ballot measure] on cognitive cues such as the names of individuals supporting or opposing a measure...." 599 F. Supp. 2d at 1208. But can voters use the name of an individual donating $100 to a ballot committee as a credible voting cue? And if there is a chance that small donors may face some retaliation, even if it does not reach the level of harassment and threats faced by the Socialist Workers Party, won't that discourage some from participating in the political process? The threat of such political chill, made more serious by the broad and immediate disclosure through user-friendly websites, might be sufficient to cause a court to question low disclosure thresholds that do not produce informational benefits.

However, the district court judge in *ProtectMarriage.com* held, in the context of the request for a preliminary injunction, that the $100 threshold in California was narrowly tailored. He noted that to hold otherwise would draw into question "scores of statutes in which the legislature or the people have sought to draw similar lines." *Id.* at 1220 (noting also that only six states have higher thresholds and that laws range from no threshold to $300). While it may be constitutional to require disclosure of contributions to ballot measures or candidates as low as $100, is it good policy? What helpful information to voters does this level of detail provide? Does it threaten instead to deluge voters with so much information that they cannot distinguish credible voting cues from mere "noise"?

How could disclosure statutes be better designed to achieve important informational objectives while also protecting the identity of people making minimal contributions to ballot measures or candidates? Not only could thresholds that trigger disclosure be raised (and perhaps indexed for inflation), but information provided in aggregate form might be more helpful for voters seeking to make competent decisions. Government officials might provide information about the occupations of donors on each side or their general locations (zip codes or in-state versus out-of-state) but not information that can be used to identify particular small donors.[b] In addition, voters might be interested in the proportion of small donors involved in any campaign, a cue that could signal grassroots support of a particular position. As lawmakers consider the right design of a new disclosure regime, they should keep in mind that distinctions can be made between information provided to government regulators, justified by the need to enforce other campaign regulations, and information disseminated broadly. Thresholds trig-

---

    b. See Scott M. Noveck, *Campaign Finance Disclosure and the Legislative Process*, 47 Harv. J. on Legis. 75 (2010).

gering requirements that information be provided to regulators might be lower than those triggering the wider disclosure. See Richard Briffault, *Campaign Finance Disclosure 2.0*, 9 Election L.J. ___ (forthcoming 2010).

The second case implicating disclosure and direct democracy was decided by the Supreme Court in June 2010. Again, the context was the emotional issue of the rights accorded to same-sex couples, and again one of the plaintiffs was a group affiliated with the Protect Marriage organization.

Doe v. Reed, 130 S.Ct. 2811 (2010). The Washington Public Records Act (PRA) requires disclosure of all public records, including referendum petitions. Petitions include the names and addresses of the people who sign them. In 2009, Protect Marriage Washington circulated a petition to overturn a law that provided substantial rights to domestic partners. When the petitions were turned in to the Secretary of State, several pro-gay-rights groups sought to obtain the documents under the PRA so that they could post the names and addresses of signatories on the Internet on websites called WhoSigned.org and KnowThyNeighbor.org. The referendum petition sponsor and some signers moved to enjoin the public release of documents that would reveal the names and contact information of the petition signers, claiming disclosure burdened their constitutional rights and chilled political speech.

The Supreme Court ruled that the PRA was not facially unconstitutional as it applied to the disclosure of referendum petitions, but it left open the possibility of as-applied challenges in the future. Although eight members of the Court agreed with the judgment, there were seven opinions; the concurring opinions mainly provided views about the standard to be applied in any subsequent as-applied challenges raised by these plaintiffs or others concerned about the consequences of releasing referendum petitions. In the opinion for the Court, **Chief Justice Roberts** characterized signing a petition as an expression of a political view, thus implicating the First Amendment. He found that disclosure of petitions met the "exacting scrutiny" required by the First Amendment because it assists state officials in discovering fraud and in verifying the accuracy of the signatures. The Secretary of State can only check a small fraction of signatures; disclosure "can help cure the inadequacies of the verification and canvassing process [and help] prevent certain types of petition fraud otherwise difficult to detect, such as outright forgery." He concluded that "[p]ublic disclosure also promotes transparency and accountability in the electoral process to an extent other measures cannot."

Although the Chief Justice acknowledged that these plaintiffs might be able to demonstrate a reasonable probability of threats, reprisals, and harassment—and thus avoid disclosure in this particular case—he rejected the argument that most ballot measures would give rise to such harm. He suggested that the subject matter of this measure was especially "controversial," in contrast to the typical fodder for direct democracy: tax policy, revenue and budget issues, property rights laws, and utility regulation. He noted that the plaintiffs could "press the narrower challenge" on remand. In his concurrence, **Justice Stevens** took issue with any distinction based on the subject matter of initiatives, noting that "[d]ebates about tax policy and regulation of private property can become just as heated as debates about domestic partnerships." And **Justice Thomas**, the only justice who dissented, argued that the nature of direct democracy, which operates as a "safety valve" for interests that have not succeeded in the legislature, means that many ballot measures will be controversial.

Applying strict scrutiny to the PRA and finding it constitutionally objectionable as it affected referendum petitions, **Justice Thomas** argued that the state had many other, less burdensome approaches available to detect and combat fraud in the signature-gathering process. He characterized the Washington statute as a "blunderbuss approach," noting alternatives like an electronic referendum database that could detect multiple references to a single voter and that could allow voters to search for their names to discover outright fraud. On the other side of the balance, he was concerned that as-applied challenges would not offer sufficient protection to petition signers. For example, if petition sponsors worried about backlash aimed at signers must seek an injunction before circulating petitions, how do they present sufficient evidence of a reasonable probability of threats, reprisals, and harassment? Do they have to wait until there is such retaliation and then seek protection? Moreover, Thomas argued, "the state of technology today creates at least *some* probability that signers of every referendum will be subjected to threats, harassment, or reprisals if their personal information is disclosed."

Most of the other opinions focused on providing guidance for future as-applied challenges in the age of the Internet, and the Justices disagreed about the showing that would be required for an as-applied challenge to succeed. **Justice Alito** contended that First Amendment rights are adequately protected only if an as-applied challenge could be brought "sufficiently far in advance" to avoid any political chill and "the showing necessary to obtain the exemption is not overly burdensome." As to the former, the exemption must be available before a petition is circulated so the signers will know that their identities will be protected. As to the latter, "speakers must be able to obtain an as-applied exemption without clearing a high evidentiary hurdle."

Alito went further to opine that the plaintiffs in *Doe v. Reed* had a strong case for an exemption, citing among other things the evidence of "widespread harassment and intimidation suffered by supporters of California's Proposition 8." Indicating that he might be closer to Justice Thomas' view than the majority's, Alito also disparaged the state's interest in disclosure as relatively "inadequa[te]." For example, he criticized the state's interest in providing information to voters about who is supporting a ballot measure, because he believed that would also support disclosure of a great deal of demographic information about signers such as their race, religion, and interest group memberships. He also rejected the notion that it was permissible to provide information to allow voters to contact signers and discuss the matter with them. In this case the groups seeking names were intent on having "uncomfortable conversation[s]" with the supporters of the petition, so "disclosure becomes a means of facilitating harassment." Finally, he noted that most other states, including initiative-happy California, do not require such broad disclosure of referendum petitions, and it was only a recent development in Washington that occurred as part of a broader open records movement. Apparently, other methods are sufficient to meet most states' concerns about fraud.

In contrast, **Justice Sotomayor** and **Justice Stevens** both wrote separately to underscore their views that the standard of proof to obtain an exemption from disclosure should be rigorous. Disclosure is a long-accepted mechanism to protect the integrity of the electoral process; citizens signing petitions do so in public without a guarantee of confidentiality; and there is little, if any, evidence that disclosing the names of signers causes people to be less willing to sign a petition. Justice Sotomayor counseled that "courts * * * should be deeply skeptical of any assertion that the Constitution, which embraces political transparency, compels States to conceal the identity of persons who seek to participate in lawmaking through a state-created referendum process." Justice Stevens put it differently: For a successful as-applied challenge, "there would have to be a significant threat of harassment that cannot be mitigated by law enforcement measures."

Justice Scalia took a unique approach to the case, rejecting the initial conclusion that signing a petition implicated the First Amendment. His originalist approach included discussion of the history of voting in the U.S., which was not done by secret ballot until the late 19th century and was not justified then as a move compelled by the Constitution. He also noted that the initiative process grew out of town hall meetings and the right to petition the government for change—both of these activities were done in public. Indeed, he viewed direct democracy as lawmaking, and "[t]he public nature of federal lawmaking is constitutionally required" by, among other things, Article I, § 5, cl. 3 of the Constitution that requires each house of Congress to keep a Journal of Proceedings. He concluded: "There are laws against threats and intimidation; and harsh criticism, short of unlawful action, is a price our people have traditionally been willing to pay for self-governance. Requiring people to stand up in public for their political acts fosters civic courage, without which democracy is doomed."

What does *Doe v. Reed* mean for further proceedings in *ProtectMarriage.com*? What is the right standard for a court to apply when asked for an as-applied exemption from disclosure in cases like these? How does new technology affect the balance under the First Amendment? What other issues are likely to spark litigation in this realm?

CHAPTER 7

THEORIES OF STATUTORY INTERPRETATION

■ ■ ■

SECTION 3. CURRENT DEBATES IN STATUTORY INTERPRETATION

A. THE NEW TEXTUALISM

Page 798. Insert the following Cases, Article, and Notes at the end of Part A, following the Query:

PORTLAND GENERAL ELECTRIC CO. v. BUREAU OF LABOR AND INDUSTRIES

Court of Appeals of Oregon, 1992
116 Or.App. 356, 842 P.2d 419

DE MUNIZ, J.

Petitioner seeks review of an order of the Commissioner of the Bureau of Labor and Industries (BOLI) that held that petitioner had engaged in an unlawful employment practice. ORS 659.360. It assigns error to BOLI's conclusion that an employee was entitled to use his accrued paid sick leave as parental leave, even though he was not "sick" within the definition of his employment agreement or company policy. We affirm.

The employee is a service inspector and a member of the International Brotherhood of Electrical Workers (IBEW). In March, 1988, he requested 12 weeks of parental leave, composed of two weeks of accrued vacation leave, three days of accrued sick leave available for elective surgery and nine weeks and two days of other accrued sick leave. Petitioner denied the request, because the collective bargaining agreement in effect between petitioner and IBEW provides that sick leave is to be used only when an employee is actually sick or injured. Petitioner later granted the employee's amended request for 10 weeks of parental leave, which substituted seven weeks and two days unpaid leave for the nine weeks and two days paid sick leave.

BOLI's decision was based on ORS 659.360(3), which provides:

"The employee seeking parental leave *shall be entitled to utilize any accrued* vacation leave, *sick leave* or other compensatory leave, paid or unpaid, *during the parental leave.* The employer may require the employee seeking parental leave to utilize any accrued leave during the parental leave unless otherwise provided by an agreement of the employer and the employee, by collective bargaining agreement or by employer policy." (Emphasis supplied.)

Petitioner argues that the emphasized language means that an employee may use paid sick leave during parental leave only if the employee is sick, as defined by the collective bargaining agreement. BOLI concluded that the employee's right to take that leave is not subject to the preconditions for use of sick leave contained in the collective bargaining agreement.

We begin with the language of the statute. It says that an employee "shall be entitled to utilize *any accrued* * * * sick leave * * * during the parental leave." (Emphasis supplied.)

"Entitled to utilize" must mean "has a right to use." The only limit on that right to use sick leave during a parental leave is that the leave have accrued. Period. The provision simply says that, if the leave is accrued, the employee has a right to use it during the parental leave. That should be the end to a simple statutory question.

However, petitioner argues, and the dissenters agree, that the right to use paid sick leave during the parental leave is subject to the preconditions for use of the leave provided in the collective bargaining agreement. The easy answer to that contention is that the statute does not include that limitation, and we are not at liberty to add it. ORS 174.010. In addition, careful review of the statutory language, both in isolation and in context, leads inescapably to the conclusion that that interpretation is inconsistent with legislative intent.

The sole modifier before "vacation leave" and "sick leave" is "accrued." That modifier has a definite meaning in the employment context. As the *amicus* brief so ably explains, there is a difference between "accrued" leave, which is the maturation or vesting of the right to a benefit, usually based on completion of periods of employment; "eligibility" for leave or other benefits, which is the meeting of the threshold legal requirements, such as permanent employment versus temporary employment; and "entitlement" to use benefits, which is the result of fulfillment of preconditions to use, such as illness in the case of sick leave. By providing a single precondition for use of sick leave during parental leave, that the leave have *accrued*, the legislature did *not* limit the use of that leave to sick leave the employee would otherwise be entitled to use under a collective bargaining agreement.[5]

Furthermore, the contrast between the two sentences in subsection (3) makes it patently clear that the employee's right to use accrued sick

---

5. When the legislature intended collective bargaining agreements to govern in the Parental Leave Law, it specifically said so. [E.g., ORS 659.360(3) (second sentence), and .360(6) (quoted in text).]

leave is not otherwise limited by the collective bargaining agreement. The first sentence, which sets out the *employee*'s right to use accrued leave, does not refer to employment agreements:

> "The employee seeking parental leave *shall be entitled to utilize any accrued* vacation leave, *sick leave* or other compensatory leave, paid or unpaid, *during the parental leave.*" (Emphasis supplied.)

In contrast, the second sentence says:

> "The employer may require the employee seeking parental leave to utilize any accrued leave during the parental leave *unless otherwise provided by an agreement of the employer and the employee, by collective bargaining agreement or by employer policy.*" (Emphasis supplied.)

Thus, the *employer's* right to require an employee to use accrued leave is specifically limited by any contrary agreement. When the legislature includes limiting language in one sentence of a subsection and excludes it in another, we can divine an intent that the limitation apply only as specified.

Our reading of ORS 659.360(3) comports with ORS 659.360(6):

> "The parental leave required by subsection (1) of this section is not required to be granted with pay unless so specified by agreement of the employer and employee, by collective bargaining agreement or by employer policy."

The subsection shows the distinction between a new kind of mandated leave, parental leave, and other types of leave that an employee may have accrued. Although parental leave *per se* need not be paid, an employee is entitled to use other types of leave, paid or unpaid, during the 12–week parental leave period. Subsection (6) makes clear that an employer need not provide a *new* type of *paid* leave in addition to the other types of leave already provided, unless required by an employment agreement. Regardless of the employment agreement, however, the employer must allow an employee a 12–week period for parental leave, which is unpaid unless the employee has accrued other paid leave *that the employee elects to take or that the employer requires the employee to take* during that period.

Finally, to the extent that there is any ambiguity, the legislative history supports BOLI's and our reading. The original draft of the bill provided that "[t]he leave required by subsection (1) of this Act may be unpaid leave or any other leave the employer and employee agree upon or any leave specified or allowed by any collective bargaining agreement." That language was changed to say: "The leave, with preference given to accumulated sick leave and vacation leave, required by subsection (1) of this section may be paid or unpaid leave or any other leave the employer and employee agree upon or any leave specified or allowed by any collective bargaining agreement." Finally, that subsection was changed and subsection (6) added, to read essentially as it now reads. Representative Kopetski explained that the final change was to clarify the meaning in the second version:

> "The second change is * * * to clarify, * * * to make certain that any sick leave, vacation leave, that will run *concurrently* with the 12 weeks. *And so this 12 weeks is not added on to any vacation time or sick leave that the individual would have.*" Tape Recording, House Committee on Labor, March 18, 1987, Tape 61, Side B. (Emphasis supplied.)

The language of the first draft allowed the leave to be unpaid *unless* otherwise agreed. Under the second draft language, the legislature indicated a preference for accumulated sick leave and vacation leave, *or* any other leave agreed on by the employer and employee. Clearly, it was anticipated that the employee would use accumulated sick and vacation leave during the parental leave, *i.e.*, concurrently with, rather than as a replacement for, the mandated leave. The changes in the final draft added the employer's right to *require* the employee to use that leave, if the employee did not elect to do so, in order to prevent extended absences beyond 12 weeks. It also clarified that the legislature did not intend a newly mandated paid parental leave, but that an employment agreement could provide for paid parental leave.

A careful reading of the Parental Leave Law persuades us that the legislature found a balance between the employee's need for time off to care for new family members during the critical first weeks and the employer's need for a stable work force. The law provides that an employee must be granted up to 12 weeks leave, if requested, and can elect to use any accrued leave, paid or unpaid, during that 12–week period. On the other hand, if the employee does not make the election to use accrued leave, the employer can force the employee to use the leave, subject to any agreement limiting that right. The purpose was to eliminate the danger that the employee might take 12 weeks of unpaid parental leave, during which time a replacement might need to be found, and then might seek to tack on a period thereafter in which the employee would use other accrued leave, necessitating additional replacement. The statutory scheme assures the employer that the employee is entitled to be gone 12 weeks at the maximum, and not 12 weeks in addition to any other accrued leave that the employee might be entitled to take.

The dissenters would rewrite the statute to say:

> "The employee seeking parental leave *may* use any accrued * * * sick leave * * * during the parental leave, *if the employee would be entitled otherwise to use that leave as specified in an agreement of the employer and the employee, a collective bargaining agreement or by employer policy.*"

In other words, they would engraft the qualification contained in the second sentence of subsection (3) onto the first sentence. The statute imposes no such qualification; the legislature chose clear, strong, compulsory language to assure that accrued leave, paid or unpaid, would be available for employees' use during parental leave. The qualification that the dissents propose is not in the statute, and this court cannot rewrite legislation in accordance with a policy choice that it may think is appropriate. ORS 174.010. That policy choice is for the legislature, not for the courts. * * *

JOSEPH, C.J., dissenting (joined by two other Judges). * * *

* * * [The Court holds] that the accrued sick leave may be used *as* paid parental leave. The statute simply does not say that. It says that the accrued sick leave may be used *during* the parental leave. Nothing in the language of the statute even remotely suggests that accrued sick leave may be applied to a kind of leave other than the one for which it *has accrued* simply by reason of a happenstance that the employee is enjoying a different kind of leave while some of the accrued sick time remains. * * *

EDMONDS, J., dissenting (joined by CHIEF JUSTICE JOSEPH).

I suggest that ORS 659.360(3) is, on its face, equally susceptible to the interpretations proposed by the majority and Chief Judge Joseph in his dissent. What persuades me that the legislature intended that the terms of a collective bargaining agreement control over the election of an employee are the previous drafts of the statute. There is a consistent thread in them that the legislature intended parental leave to be unpaid unless otherwise agreed by the employer and employee or unless controlled by a collective bargaining agreement. The collective bargaining agreement controls.

The majority concedes that the final draft was not intended to change the meaning of the statute but to clarify it so that the parental leave would not be added to any vacation or sick leave. That change created the ambiguity that is at the heart of the dispute over the meaning of the statute but did not change what the legislature intended. Both sentences in ORS 659.360(3) must be read together in the light of the legislative history. When that is done, it is apparent that BOLI erred when it held that petitioner had engaged in an unlawful employment practice when it adhered to the terms of the collective bargaining agreement.

PORTLAND GENERAL ELECTRIC CO. v. BUREAU OF LABOR AND INDUSTRIES

Supreme Court of Oregon, 1993
317 Or. 606, 859 P.2d 1143

VAN HOOMISSEN, J. * * *

[The Supreme Court of Oregon unanimously affirmed the Court of Appeals. Justice Van Hoomissen's opinion started with a statement of the interpretive approach Oregon courts are supposed to follow.] In interpreting a statute, the court's task is to discern the intent of the legislature. ORS 174.020. To do that, the court examines both the text and context of the statute. That is the first level of our analysis.

In this first level of analysis, the text of the statutory provision itself is the starting point for interpretation and is the best evidence of the legislature's intent. In trying to ascertain the meaning of a statutory provision, and thereby to inform the court's inquiry into legislative intent, the court considers rules of construction of the statutory text that bear directly on how to read the text. Some of those rules are mandated by statute, including, for example, the statutory enjoinder "not to insert what has been omitted, or to omit what has been inserted." ORS 174.010. Others are found in the case law, including, for example, the rule that words of common usage typically should be given their plain, natural, and ordinary meaning.

Also at the first level of analysis, the court considers the context of the statutory provision at issue, which includes other provisions of the same statute and other related statutes. Just as with the court's consideration of the text of a statute, the court utilizes rules of construction that bear directly on the interpretation of the statutory provision in context. Some of those rules are mandated by statute, including, for example, the principles that "where there are several provisions or particulars such construction is, if possible, to be adopted as will give effect to all," ORS 174.010, and that "a particular intent shall control a general one that is inconsistent with it," ORS 174.020. Other such rules of construction are found in case law, including, for example, the rules that use of a term in one section and not in another section of the same statute indicates a purposeful omission, and that use of the same term throughout a statute indicates that the term has the same meaning throughout the statute.

If the legislature's intent is clear from the above-described inquiry into text and context, further inquiry is unnecessary.

If, but only if, the intent of the legislature is not clear from the text and context inquiry, the court will then move to the second level, which is to consider legislative history to inform the court's inquiry into legislative intent. When the court reaches legislative history, it considers it along with text and context to determine whether all of those together make the legislative intent clear. If the legislative intent is clear, then the court's inquiry into legislative intent and the meaning of the statute is at an end and the court interprets the statute to have the meaning so determined.

If, after consideration of text, context, and legislative history, the intent of the legislature remains unclear, then the court may resort to general maxims of statutory construction to aid in resolving the remaining uncertainty. Although some of those maxims of statutory construction may be statutory, *see, e.g.,* ORS 174.030 (natural rights), others more commonly may be found in case law. Those include, for example, the maxim that, where no legislative history exists, the court will attempt to determine how the legislature would have intended the statute to be applied had it considered the issue. * * *

[Applying this structure to the issue on appeal, the court went no further than step one.] Both of the sentences in ORS 659.360(3) are *empowerment* sentences. The second sentence *empowers* the employer to compel an employee taking parental leave "to utilize any accrued leave."

Thus, if an employee has accrued leave, the employer could require the employee to utilize that accrued leave during the parental leave, "unless otherwise provided by an agreement of the employer and the employee, by collective bargaining agreement or by employer policy." ORS 659.360(3).

The reciprocal power, granted to the employee by the first sentence of ORS 659.360(3), permits the employee, at the employee's option, to do what the employer may require the employee to do. The employee may require the employer to let the employee "utilize" any accrued vacation leave, sick leave or other compensatory leave, paid or unpaid, during the parental leave. As noted, the first sentence of the statute does not contain any limitation on the employee's rights imposed under the provisions of a collective bargaining agreement.

In sum, the employer may *require* the employee seeking parental leave to utilize any accrued leave during parental leave, unless otherwise provided by an agreement of the employer and the employee, by collective bargaining agreement, or by employer policy, even if the employee is not on vacation or sick or does not wish to use accrued leave during the parental leave. Similarly, the employee may *require* the employer to let the employee utilize any accrued vacation leave, sick leave, or other compensatory leave, paid or unpaid during the parental leave, even if the employee is not on vacation or sick, and even if the employer does not want to do so. If the legislature had wanted to make the use of accrued leave during parental leave subject to any preconditions in an existing collective bargaining agreement, it easily could have done so by including in the first sentence of ORS 659.360(3) the same qualifying language that presently is found only in the second sentence of that subsection. The legislature knows how to include qualifying language in a statute when it wants to do so. It did not do so here. * * *

NOTE ON METHODOLOGICAL STARE DECISIS

An important feature of the Oregon Supreme Court's opinion is its effort to give *stare decisis* effect to methodological precedents like *PGE*. The House of Lords in the United Kingdom gives *stare decisis* effect to methodological precedents, and Sydney Foster argues that the U.S. Supreme Court should do the same. See Sydney Foster, *Should Courts Give* Stare Decisis *Effect to Statutory Interpretation Methodology?*, 96 Geo. L.J. 1863 (2008). Consider the values of *stare decisis*: judicial economy, predictability, and reliance interests. Foster argues that consistent treatment in matters of methodology would serve those interests—so courts should follow that practice.

On the other hand, are the reliance interests so strong in matters of methodological *stare decisis*? Is *stare decisis* as desirable or even workable for legal *standards* as it is for legal *rules*? Compare Foster, *supra*, at 1901–05 (on the whole, yes), with Connor Raso & William Eskridge, Jr., Chevron *as a Canon, Not a Precedent: An Empirical Analysis of What Motivates Justices in Agency Deference Cases*, 110 Colum. L. Rev. (forthcoming 2010) (on the whole, no).

Note, finally, that Oregon's *PGE* experiment in methodological *stare decisis* has been successful in some ways, but not in others. The following article examines the *PGE* experiment, which has seen a few unexpected twists in the new millennium. Once you have read Professor Gluck's article, reflect on the debate between Sydney Foster and her critics. Also reflect on this question: Did the Oregon Supreme Court reach the right result in *PGE*? Or have the justices strong-armed a statutory text to yield a liberal interpretation inconsistent with reliance interests? (We shall pose further questions in the notes following the Gluck article.)

Abbe Gluck, *The States as Laboratories of Statutory Interpretation: Methodological Consensus and the New Modified Textualism*, 119 Yale L.J. 1750 (2010).[1] "The vast majority of statutory interpretation theory is based on a strikingly small slice of American jurisprudence, the mere two percent of litigation that takes place in our federal courts—and, really, only the less-than-one percent of that litigation that the U.S. Supreme Court decides. The remaining ninety-eight percent of cases are heard in the netherworld of the American legal system, the state courts. And yet it would likely surprise most academics and many judges to learn that, while academics have spent the past decade speculating about the 'posttextualist era,' or the utility of congressionally legislated rules of interpretation, or the capacity of judges on multimember courts to agree on a single set of interpretive rules, many state courts have been engaging in real-world applications of precisely these concepts.

"Several state courts have implemented formalistic interpretive frameworks that govern all statutory questions. Methodological *stare decisis*—the practice of giving precedential effect to judicial statements about methodology—is generally absent from the jurisprudence of mainstream federal statutory interpretation, but appears to be a common feature of some states' statutory case law. Every state legislature in the nation has enacted certain rules of interpretation, which some state courts are, in an unexpected twist, flouting. * * * Justice Scalia's textualist statutory interpretation methodology has taken startlingly strong hold in some states, although in a form of which the Justice himself might not approve. Clearly, these developments are relevant to the mainstream debates about predictability and methodological choice, and yet federal scholars and jurists have hardly noticed them."

The state cases surveyed in Professor Gluck's article illustrate that the critical wars in statutory interpretation are far from over—and that the most interesting situs of those debates is in state rather than federal courts. Professor Gluck then provides an in-depth examination of the practice in five states—Oregon, Connecticut, Texas, Wisconsin, and Michigan—where judges take methodological *stare decisis* seriously and have

---

1. Copyright © Professor Abbe Gluck. Reprinted with permission.

adopted approaches grappling with the challenges posed by the new textualism.

"Not incidentally, these state efforts also respond directly to the leading academic proposals advanced to make federal statutory interpretation more determinate. Legislated interpretive rules, suggested in one prominent proposal, do not appear to be the answer, given the number of courts already actively resisting them. The resulting interbranch power struggles, in turn, raise new questions about separation of powers in statutory interpretation, shifting the debate away from what has been the prevailing question—which methodology best respects the respective roles of court and legislature—to the entirely different question of which branch gets to choose it.

"Another path to determinacy, however, long thought remote, now seems more possible in light of the state experiences. These state supreme courts have exercised interpretive leadership: they have imposed, both on themselves and on their subordinate courts, controlling interpretive frameworks for all statutory questions. This is a powerful counter-paradigm to that of the U.S. Supreme Court, where persistent interpretive divides and a refusal to treat methodological statements as precedential have made interpretive consensus seem impossible. Indeed, methodology seems to be an entirely different animal in these state courts. In these states, it *is* possible for one judge to bind another judge's methodological choice. And in fact, federal judges, too, readily assent to this conception of methodology in other areas of law, like contract interpretation. Yet these principles have failed to translate to the federal statutory interpretation context, without much explanation of why statutory interpretation should be any different.

"The mainstream statutory interpretation scholarship, too, may be overstating the intractability of methodological divides and the 'softness' of interpretive methodology. Its near-exclusive focus on U.S. Supreme Court cases is the culprit: the Court's often-divisive statutory cases (and personalities) have become the theoretical paradigm. * * * In less politically charged cases, consistent methodological rules may make the interpretive process more predictable, performing a coordinating function for the many parties affected—legislators who must negotiate and draft statutes, citizens who must act and litigate under them, and lower courts that must interpret them. There also are important expressive and fairness values attendant to having judges agree in advance on the nature of the project and decide all litigants' cases using the same legal principles. The state cases challenge the prevailing theoretical resistance to these concepts and highlight the possibility that, even putting the Court aside, many lower courts (both state and federal) might be receptive to consistent methodological frameworks, and that, in fact, more courts than we realize already may be implementing them.

"Finally, the state cases also challenge prevailing assumptions about textualism, the text-centric methodology that, despite its significant impact on modern statutory interpretation, has failed to emerge as the dominant methodology in the U.S. Supreme Court's interpretive battles. Of late, debates have raged in the academy over whether a methodological compromise between textualists and purposivists is possible. The prognosis has been pessimistic, as most scholars have assumed that textualism is too rigid a methodology to be the basis of a broader consensus that also includes nontextualists and, alternatively, that the textualists themselves will not bend to meet other judges halfway. But in the states studied, textualism is more than merely alive and well; it is the *controlling* interpretive approach—the consensus methodology chosen by the courts. That said, this state textualism is clearly not identical to its federal model. It is instead, I argue, a compromise version of textualism, what might be called 'modified textualism,' a theory that retains the fundamental text-first formalism of traditional textualism and yet still appears multitextured enough to offer a middle way in the methodological wars. * * *

"Modified textualism has two salient differences from the original: it ranks interpretive tools in a clear order—textual analysis, then legislative history, then default judicial presumptions—and it includes legislative history in the hierarchy. The individual components here are not new. Many jurists (though it has been assumed, not many self-proclaimed textualists) employ such a text-plus-legislative history approach. But what is new is the 'tiering' concept and the order itself. The strict hierarchy emphasizes textual analysis (step one); limits the use of legislative history (only in step two, and only if textual analysis alone does not suffice); and dramatically reduces reliance on the oft-used policy presumptions, the 'substantive canons' of interpretation (only in step three, and only if all else fails).

"To be sure, some textualist purists might not consider this theory 'textualist' at all. Textualists generally have eschewed use of legislative history and do widely employ the substantive canons. Such a rush to judgment against modified textualism, however, would be a mistake. These state cases illustrate both that traditional textualist theory is capacious enough to accommodate this moderate heterogeneity and that, in fact, this accommodation may be textualism's best chance to accomplish its core theoretical goal of implementing a predictable, text-centric approach to interpretation.

"And because this methodology is the basis for broader agreement in the states studied, it also has implications for purposivism, the other dominant modern theory, and the broader literature about methodological compromise. Purposivists typically embrace a more flexible approach, an approach from which modified textualism's strict interpretive hierarchy is a departure. But, arguably, modified textualism offers purposivists what might be called a more 'disciplined' version of their current method—a way to legitimize the use of legislative history and concretize their approach so that it can be applied consistently, and repeatedly, by lower courts. It is intriguing to see at least some purposivist judges attracted to this structured approach—an approach that, unlike other compromise proposals advanced in the scholarship, still appeals to textualism on its own theoretical terms.

"The five states chosen for focused study—Oregon, Connecticut, Texas, Wisconsin and Michigan—were chosen following a preliminary review of state statutory interpretation across the highest courts of all fifty states and the District of Columbia, and they were selected because their interpretive moves were particularly explicit, both in terms of clearly identifiable interpretive developments underway and the extensive discussions, in the cases themselves, of those developments. My initial focus was on identifying courts with internal divides over methodological choice and states in which the legislatures had passed laws concerning interpretive rules. Texas and Connecticut were chosen once it became apparent that both states' courts, despite different methodological preferences, were engaged in similar dialogues with their legislatures over which branch controls the rules of interpretation. Michigan and Wisconsin were originally chosen because those states' supreme courts are internally divided and methodological choice is often heatedly debated in opinions. Oregon was chosen simply because of the surprise of identifying a sixteen-year controlling interpretive regime that has gone virtually unnoticed by the academy. My aims in state selection, moreover, did not include identifying methodological *stare decisis*, consensus regimes, or modified textualism. The state courts' convergences on those themes emerged, and subsequently became the focus of the Article, only after I had selected the states and completed a deeper analysis of their case law. The five states are also geographically and demographically diverse and employ different methods of judicial selection. * * *

"In 1993, the Oregon Supreme Court took the problem of interpretive choice into its own hands. In the watershed case, *Portland General Electric v. Bureau of Labor and Industries (PGE)*, the court unanimously announced a three-step methodology to control all future statutory interpretation questions. Even more notably, the new methodological regime stuck. The court not only applied the methodology 'religiously' in the sixteen years following its announcement, it did so without a single dissenting opinion from any member of that court arguing the methodology did not control as a matter of *stare decisis*. *PGE* 'is the single most frequently cited case decision in the state's history.' The announced methodology even remained controlling despite legislation enacted in 2001 aimed at overruling part of it. Indeed, it was not until April 2009—eight years after the legislation was enacted—that the Oregon court even was willing to consider whether the legislature could amend the court-imposed framework.

"The *PGE* case and its implications for interpretive indeterminacy have gone completely unnoticed outside of Oregon. The case and its progeny offer a perhaps unparalleled example of a judicially imposed, consistently applied interpretive regime for statutory cases that has remained in place unaltered for a sixteen-year period For this reason, it is worth bracketing for a moment the Oregon Supreme Court's recent opinion concerning the legislative attempt to amend *PGE* (which muddies the waters somewhat), and examining in detail the three-step *PGE* test. * * *

"The Oregon Framework not only lists relevant interpretive factors, it orders and ranks them. As *PGE* held:

[1] In this first level of analysis, the text of the statutory provision itself is the starting point for interpretation. . . . In trying to ascertain the meaning of a statutory provision . . . the court considers rules of construction of the statutory text that bear directly on how to read the text . . . for example, the statutory enjoinder "not to insert what has been omitted, or to omit what has been inserted." . . .

Also at the first level of analysis, the court considers the context of the statutory provision at issue, which includes other provisions of the same statute and other related statutes. . . .

[2] *If, but only if*, the intent of the legislature is not clear from the text and context inquiry, the court will then move to the second level, which is to consider legislative history. . . . If the legislative intent is clear, then the court's inquiry into legislative intent . . . is at an end. . . .

[3] If, after consideration of text, context, and legislative history, the intent of the legislature remains unclear, then the court may resort to general maxims of statutory construction to aid in resolving the remaining uncertainty.

"Although the *PGE* framework gives text precedence, it is decidedly different from Justice Scalia's textualism. *PGE*'s first, text-only, tier would certainly appeal to textualists. The Oregon Supreme Court made clear that the only interpretive rules permitted in this first step are the so-called 'textual' canons, which 'assist the statutory interpreter in deriving probable meaning from the four corners of the statutory text.' If the textual aids do not achieve clarity, however, the *PGE* framework mandates an antitextualist turn: legislative history is the second step of the inquiry. Only where ambiguity persists after consideration of text and legislative history, does the Oregon court allow for resort to all the remaining 'general maxims of statutory construction.'

"Textualists in Justice Scalia's vein would not look to legislative history in any event and often *do* consider the various substantive canons of interpretation that the Oregon court considers 'general maxims,' including the rule of lenity and the canon of constitutional avoidance. In contrast, Oregon has significantly diminished the importance of these canons by relegating them to the third tier of the *PGE* analysis. The *PGE* framework has caused the near-elimination of the rule of lenity and the canon of constitutional avoidance from Oregon Supreme Court cases. In addition, Oregon's highest court has expressly excluded from the 'level one' textual analysis the rule against absurdities. That rule has been the main escape valve for Scalia-style textualists, who invoke it to justify departure from clear statutory text if a literal reading would work absurd results. The Oregon Court's rationale for demoting the rule—'we would be rewriting a clear statute based solely on our conjecture that the legislature should not have intended a particular result'—echoes the main criticism that academics have levied at the textualist jurists on the federal side who still employ the canon, and also upends some academic assumptions that courts would never compromise on a text-based methodology without that escape valve.

"*PGE* also differs from purposivism or a more eclectic approach. The test's tiered hierarchy is strict: it prioritizes text over purpose in all situations, prohibits consultation of legislative history absent a threshold finding of ambiguity, and eschews an all-things-considered approach in favor of a formalized step-by-step process. Indeed, the Oregon Supreme Court devised the *PGE* regime at least partially in direct response to the uncertainty occasioned by the federal courts' eclectic approach.

"Three preliminary studies, including one conducted as part of this project, have collected data on how the *PGE* regime has been implemented since its installation. One clearly observable effect of the regime is that it has reduced the number of interpretive tools employed by the Oregon Supreme Court and so made it easier to predict which tools the court will rely on to decide cases. 'The court resolves the vast majority of statutory issues at level one,' i.e., the text-based tier. Between 1993 and 1998, for example, out of 137 statutory interpretation cases, the court looked at legislative history only thirty-three times, finding it 'useless' in one third of those cases. It consequently reached tier three—nontextual canons— only eleven times during the same period. Even more strikingly, between 1999 and 2006, the court applied the *PGE* framework 150 times, and only reached tier two (legislative history) nine times. Not a single case during that period reached the other-maxims tier (tier three). And, in a study conducted as part of this project, across the thirty-five cases in which *PGE* was cited between 2006 and May 2009, legislative history was applied six times and a substantive canon only once.

"Compare the five years before *PGE* was decided. There was no single approach: more than half of the cases resorted immediately to legislative history or policy analysis without prior consideration of text alone, and without the tiered hierarchy of sources that *PGE* later imposed. One justice called the pre-*PGE* period a 'legislative history free-for-all.'

"In contrast, under *PGE*, the court is fairly consistent with respect to which interpretive tools it relies upon. Over the four-and-a-half year period ending in May 2009, the following eight types of textual tools were used in roughly half of the cases: 'plain meaning,' dictionaries, state court precedents, close readings of statutory definition sections, analysis of related statutes, analysis of the contested term's place in the statutory scheme, historical evolution of the statute itself, and textual canons. With respect to the textual canons, the court applied the same eight canons repeatedly throughout the cases in which textual canons were used. The only additional tools used in more than three cases were rules of grammar (ten cases) and legislative history (nine cases), making the list of the eight types of tools described above the fairly complete universe of Oregon statutory interpretation principles. All but six of the opinions over the five-year period were unanimous.

"Moreover, all of the Oregon judges and justices agree that *PGE*'s application is mandatory. Even those Oregon judges who disagree with aspects of the framework, or the results dictated by it in particular cases, concede that they must use it. There are examples of cases in which legislative history likely would have dictated the opposite result, but the Oregon courts confined themselves to a different, text-based decision because of *PGE*. The framework survived the turnover of almost the entire state supreme court; only one justice who was on the court when *PGE* was decided remains. Litigants tailor their briefs to match the three-step regime. * * *

"While the idea of a single interpretive regime appears to have taken firm root in Oregon, what that regime should look like remains a live issue. In 2001, the Oregon legislature enacted a statute in direct response to *PGE*. The statute stated: 'A court may limit its consideration of legislative history to the information that the parties provide to the court. A court shall give the weight to the legislative history that the court considers to be appropriate.' Although on its face, the statute does not appear to contradict *PGE*, the legislative history (ironically) makes clear that the bill 'addresses the Oregon Supreme Court's three-level approach to statutory interpretation as announced in [*PGE*],' was enacted with the purpose of bringing legislative history into the first tier of analysis, and would 'allow a party to offer legislative history to the court to aid in its pursuit of the legislature's intent, regardless of whether the meaning of a statute is clear from its text and context.'

"For eight years, the Oregon Supreme Court refused to even acknowledge the possibility that the statute amended the *PGE* test. Instead, it ignored litigants' repeated requests that the supreme court apply it, and adhered to its three-step regime. As a result, the lower state courts consistently read the statute as in conflict with *PGE* and so refused to give the statute any effect. Every court to consider the issue—including the Ninth Circuit—assumed that *PGE* controlled and so refused to even consider legislative history in Oregon cases if the text was clear.

"All the more puzzling, then, is what happened next. In a case decided in April 2009, *Gaines v. State*, the Oregon Supreme Court unexpectedly requested briefing on the relevance of the statute. The ensuing decision—even as the opinion insists that *PGE* still governs—contains confusing language about when the court will now consider legislative history. The court held that *PGE*'s text-only first step remains the same but that the parties are free to 'proffer' legislative history, and that the court will consult it regardless of ambiguity, but only 'where that legislative history appears useful.' The court also held, however, that even clear contradictory evidence of purpose will not trump plain text. The opinion left many open questions, and it is too soon to predict its lasting effect, but one immediate effect is remarkable: fifteen of the sixteen Oregon Supreme Court cases that since have cited *Gaines* looked to legislative history—a dramatic turnaround from the near-disappearance of legislative history use in the state under *PGE*. * * *

"The *PGE* test might prove to be an enduring framework or only a sixteen-year experiment. But, either way, the Oregon Supreme Court's experience with it refutes the claim, made in the mainstream scholarship, that methodological consensus is impossible. What the court did was more than just articulate a preferred standard; it applied it in virtually all statutory cases. What's more, it appears to have applied it with a fair degree of consistency, creating a small and predictable universe of interpretive tools, producing very few intracourt fights about whether cases are to be decided at step one, two, or three, and giving rise to apparently not a single dissenting or concurring opinion claiming the court was manipulating its methodological framework to reach preferred results. Indeed, although *Gaines* may ultimately change what the controlling framework looks like, it will not change the more important development from a theoretical standpoint, namely, that the Oregon Supreme Court remains committed to having a single approach for all statutory questions and treats its methodological statements as binding precedents."

Professor Gluck examines the different experiments in **Texas**, where the Supreme Court has applied a strict plain meaning rule and excluded legislative history unless the statute is ambiguous (substantially ignoring a statute requiring consideration of legislative history and purpose in all cases); **Connecticut**, where the Supreme Court has rejected the plain meaning rule, see *State v. Courchesne,* 816 A.2d 562 (Ct. 2003), and has usually ignored a state statute enacted in response to *Courchesne* and seeking to re-impose the plain meaning rule; **Wisconsin**, where the Supreme Court has established a precedential regime centered around a plain meaning rule, see *Kalal v. Circuit Court,* 681 N.W.2d 110 (Wis. 2004), but one that continues to be challenged from time to time; **Michigan**, a similar story as Wisconsin, except that the plain meaning regime was supported by a 4–3 majority that may be imperiled by the electoral defeat of the Chief Justice (with a focus on this issue) in 2008.

QUO VADIS, TEXTUALISM? SOME THEORETICAL NOTES

1. *A Modified Textualism.* Professor Gluck's article celebrates *PGE* as a "modified textualism" that has greater appeal and more hope to create a stable equilibrium than Justice Scalia's new textualism. Note three differences between Oregon's approach and Justice Scalia's approach:

(A) *Legislative History.* The Oregon model retains a role for legislative history, anathema to Justice Scalia. Indeed, the role is bigger than the Oregon Supreme Court openly acknowledges. Any lawyer writing an appellate brief in Oregon must research legislative history and report anything that she believes is relevant and helpful to the case. (If counsel is 100% "certain" that the statute has a plain meaning, she might ignore it. But many a lawyer has been "certain" that one argument will prevail, thereby neglecting other arguments, and discovered with dismay that the judges did not agree. This kind of certainty may constitute malpractice.) And if judges are reading the legislative history (via the appellate briefs), is it not apparent that any judgment about "plain meaning" is one that will consider the meaning legislators thought they were writing into the statute?

The news is even worse for the new textualism at the state level. In an unpublished paper, Brian Barnes empirically demonstrates that, at the state level, much (much) more legislative history is publicly available now than ten years ago (and more was available ten years ago than 20 years ago), and much is available on-line. The greater *accessibility* of legislative history drives more briefing of legislative history by lawyers and, ultimately, greater judicial reliance on legislative history. See Brian Barnes, *The Transformation of State Statutory Interpretation* (Yale Law School, Seminar Paper, May 10, 2010). Barnes's analysis suggests that the BIG news in state statutory interpretation is neither textualism nor *stare decisis*, but rather it is the steadily increasing availability and judicial deployment of legislative history.

(B) *Substantive Canons of Statutory Construction.* The *PGE* approach preserves a potentially important role for substantive canons of statutory construction. Although Professor Gluck notes that the Oregon Supreme Court has excluded the presumption against absurd results from Step 1, it may be available at Step 3, and perhaps, after *Gaines*, this substantive canon might gravitate upwards in the court's list. Step 3 surely includes the major substantive canons—including the notions of interpreting statutes to carry out their purposes, to avoid constitutional problems, and to impose criminal liability only where the legislature has clearly targeted the defendant's conduct.

(C) *Liberal Textualism.* It is hard for us to imagine that Justice Scalia would have gone along with the Oregon Supreme Court in *PGE*, largely because the result is so pro-union and imposes new costs upon employers. Justice Scalia could dissent by invoking textualist premises. The collective bargaining agreement says an employee *cannot* take *paid* sick leave unless she/he is actually sick; ORS 659.360(6) says that parental leave need *not* be *paid* unless the collective bargaining (or some other) agreement provides for it; ORS 659.360(3) says *nothing* about whether sick leave invoked by the employee for use as parental leave must be *paid* (the sick or other compensatory leave can be either paid or unpaid). Yet the Oregon Supreme Court says that ORS 659.360(3) requires the employer to pay for most of the parental leave under the aegis of accrued sick leave, even though the collective bargaining agreement says this does not qualify as paid leave. The state parental leave statute is transformed from one where the state guarantees 12 weeks of *unpaid* leave into a statute where the state guarantees 12 weeks of largely *paid* leave. Can the language of the first sentence of ORS 659.360(3) carry the weight of this transformation? Has the Oregon Supreme Court sacrificed judicial neutrality through this exercise in dynamic textualism?

2. *No Frills Textualism.* At *PGE* Step 1, the Oregon Supreme Court says that judges should look at the structure of the statute as well as its plain meaning; when the statute is ambiguous, judges are supposed to consult legislative history (Step 2) and substantive canons (Step 3). Justice Scalia's new textualism would eliminate Step 2. His former law clerk, Professor Adrian Vermeule, argues for a much more parsimonious textualism in *Judging Under Uncertainty* (2006). Professor Vermeule's normative baseline is an institutional cost-benefit calculus: *Ex ante*, what method of statutory interpretation will minimize institutional costs, especially errors? His judgment is that judges applying the traditional, multi-factored approach (casebook, pp. 830–35) make a lot of mistakes and impose huge research costs on lawyers and their clients.

In his view, institutional costs would be lower—for both judges and for parties—if the Supreme Court trimmed away the least useful sources of statutory meaning, not only legislative history, but also arguments from statutory structure. Fewer mistakes would be made if courts deferred to agencies that understand the statute and can fill in legal gaps with expert judgments. Hence, what we have dubbed a *no frills textualism*[2] (Professor Vermeule's approach) would exclude "related statutes" from statutory meaning (pp. 202–04) and would consider only the "directly dispositive clauses or provisions at hand" (p. 204), apparently excluding most whole act analysis. Although resort to linguistic canons and some substantive canons is, concededly, inevitable (p. 200), Professor Vermeule says that agencies, not courts, should pick the canonical default rules in a systematic way before the case arises (p. 201).

How would Professor Vermeule's theory apply to *PGE*? What provisions in the labor statute would be the "directly dispositive clauses or provisions at hand"? How should the interpreter view them? If there were ambiguity (is there?), Professor Vermeule would say that BOLI (the agency litigant) should identify the canons that should govern. Assume that BOLI identified as an important canon the notion that statutes should be interpreted to carry out their liberal, pro-employee purposes. (This is quite plausible given BOLI's decision in *PGE*.) Should BOLI be able to bootstrap its pro-employee stance in this way—and make it binding on courts? Does its application to *PGE* suggest that Professor Vermeule's theory would be easy to apply?

3. *Funnel of Abstraction Textualism.* Another kind of textualist theory is the Eskridge and Frickey "Funnel of Abstraction" (casebook, pp. 830–35). The Funnel is a textualist theory, because it not only starts with the statutory text (including the statutory structure) but also considers text the weightiest factor: When it is clear, the text trumps legislative history, statutory purpose, and agency interpretations. The Funnel is a softer textualist theory, however: Professors Eskridge and Frickey never stop with the text and urge interpreters to consult other sources to make sure the text is really as "clear" as they view it on first impression *and* invite judges to adjust relatively clear texts when legislative history, statutory purpose, and public norms press strongly in the other direction.

---

2. William N. Eskridge, Jr., *No Frills Textualism*, 119 Harv. L. Rev. 2041 (2006) (reviewing Vermeule's book).

How would a judge applying the Funnel of Abstraction decide *PGE*? (To answer this question, you must examine the Court of Appeals decision as well as the Supreme Court decision in *PGE*.) By the way, Professors Eskridge and Frickey believe that the *PGE* three-tiered approach is a simpler version of the Funnel. The main articulated difference is that the *PGE* Mini-Funnel requires "ambiguity" for the interpreter to travel up the Funnel—but Eskridge and Frickey observe that any judicial judgment about plain meaning (Step 1 of *PGE*) would be made *only* after the judge has read what the briefs have to say about drafting history, legislative history and purpose, and applicable canons, and so the Funnel factors sneak into the judge's deliberation. The Oregon Supreme Court has, in *Gaines*, opened the door for this more openly.

So should state courts adopt the Funnel? Would that serve the *stare decisis* interests that Professor Gluck celebrates?

CHAPTER 8

DOCTRINES OF STATUTORY INTERPRETATION

■ ■ ■

SECTION 1. RULES, PRESUMPTIONS, AND CANONS OF STATUTORY INTERPRETATION

B. SUBSTANTIVE CANONS

1. The Rule of Lenity in Criminal Cases

Page 903. Insert the following Case and Problem right before *Davis*:

Skilling v. United States, 130 S.Ct. 2896 (2010). Founded in 1985, Enron Corporation swiftly became the seventh highest-revenue-grossing company in America. Jeffrey Skilling was a longtime Enron officer, its chief executive officer for most of 2001. Less than four months after he resigned, Enron crashed into bankruptcy, and its stock plummeted in value. After an investigation uncovered a conspiracy to prop up Enron's stock prices by overstating the company's financial well-being, the federal government prosecuted dozens of Enron employees, culminating in prosecutions of Skilling and two other top executives. The indictment charged that these three defendants violated several federal criminal statutes when they allegedly engaged in a scheme to deceive investors about Enron's true financial performance by manipulating its publicly reported financial results and making false and misleading statements. Count 1 of the indictment charged Skilling with conspiracy to commit "honest-services" wire fraud, 18 U. S. C. §§ 371, 1343, 1346, by depriving Enron and its shareholders of the intangible right of his honest services. Skilling was convicted of these and other charges, and his conviction was upheld on appeal to the Fifth Circuit.

The Supreme Court reversed Skilling's § 1346 conviction. **Justice Ginsburg**'s opinion for the Court on this issue (joined by **Chief Justice Roberts** and **Justices Stevens**, **Breyer**, **Alito**, and **Sotomayor**) interpreted § 1346 to be limited to schemes to defraud of honest services only where there have been bribes and kickbacks. Justice Ginsburg started with a review of pre–1987 mail and wire fraud prosecutions under §§ 1341 and 1343 that expanded "scheme to defraud" crimes to include losses of "honest services" and not just losses of tangible property. The leading case was *Shushan* v. *United States*, 117 F.2d 110 (5th Cir. 1941), which upheld the mail fraud prosecution of a public official who allegedly accepted bribes from entrepreneurs in exchange for urging city action beneficial to the bribe payers. "A scheme to get a public contract on more favorable terms than would likely be got otherwise by bribing a public official," the court observed, "would not only be a plan to commit the crime of bribery, but would also be a scheme to defraud the public." By 1987, every federal court of appeals had accepted the "honest services" interpretation of the mail (§ 1341) and wire (§ 1343) fraud statutes, usually in cases that involved bribes or kickbacks.

In *McNally* (casebook, pp. 898–901), the Supreme Court stopped the lower court development of the intangible rights doctrine "in its tracks"— and Congress "responded swiftly," with new § 1346 (casebook, pp. 900– 01). Skilling argued that the swift response was too vague to satisfy the Due Process Clause, however. "To satisfy due process, 'a penal statute [must] define the criminal offense [1] with sufficient definiteness that ordinary people can understand what conduct is prohibited and [2] in a manner that does not encourage arbitrary and discriminatory enforcement.' *Kolender* v. *Lawson*, 461 U.S. 352, 357 (1983)." Skilling claimed that § 1346 does not clearly define what behavior it prohibits and its "standardless sweep allows policemen, prosecutors, and juries to pursue their personal predilections," and sought a judgment invalidating the statute.

"In urging invalidation of § 1346, Skilling swims against our case law's current, which requires us, if we can, to construe, not condemn, Congress' enactments." No court of appeals had ruled that § 1346 was void for vagueness, and the Supreme Court agreed that the better path was a narrowing construction. "First we look to the doctrine developed in pre-*McNally* cases in an endeavor to ascertain the meaning of the phrase 'the intangible right of honest services.' Second, to preserve what Congress certainly intended the statute to cover, we pare that body of precedent down to its core: In the main, the pre-*McNally* cases involved fraudulent schemes to deprive another of honest services through bribes or kickbacks supplied by a third party who had not been deceived. Confined to these paramount applications, § 1346 presents no vagueness problem."

Based upon constitutional vagueness concerns and the rule of lenity in criminal cases, Justice Ginsburg rejected the government's suggestion that § 1346 also include cases where there is "undisclosed self-dealing by a public official or private employee—*i.e.*, the taking of official action by the employee that furthers his own undisclosed financial interests while purporting to act in the interests of those to whom he owes a fiduciary duty." Because Skilling's alleged misbehavior did not include charges that he received bribes or kickbacks, Justice Ginsburg reversed his § 1346 conviction and remanded to the lower courts to determine whether the other convictions could stand.

Justice Scalia (joined by **Justices Thomas** and **Kennedy**) concurred in the Court's judgment but would have declared § 1346 void for vagueness. He viewed the Court's surgery on § 1346 to be "not interpretation but invention," the equivalent of judicial crafting of a common law crime, which our nation's constitutional culture has long abjured. *E.g.*, *United States v. Hudson*, 7 Cranch 32, 34 (1812). Additionally, Justice Scalia wondered what rewritten/narrowed § 1346 now covered: Does it apply to private officials, such as Skilling, at all? What would constitute a "bribe" or "kickback" (terms that do not appear in the statute but that are now interpolated into it by the majority) in future cases?

bribe + kickback?

PROBLEM ON THE CASE OF THE FRAUDULENT INSURANCE SCHEMERS

Problem 8–1a. **Person A** is the state Commissioner of Insurance, who decides what insurance companies will receive contracts to insure certain state activities and buildings. **Person B** heads the Squalid Insurance Company, which wants to secure contracting rights to insure all state buildings associated with public education. **Person C** is a leader of the Cut–Taxes Party, which has won control of the state legislature and just elected a governor in the state. **A** switches parties to become a Cut–Taxer. In the process, **A**, **B**, and **C** enter into an agreement whereby **A** would funnel all state education insurance contracts to Squalid Insurance, which would then pay $100,000 per year to a company partly owned by **A** and would contribute $500,000 a year to the Cut–Taxes Party.

Federal investigators uncover this scheme, and prosecutors indict **A**, **B**, and **C** for violating § 1346. Each defendant argues that the statute does not apply to him or her after *Skilling*. Should any of the defendants prevail? Which one(s)?

C. DEBUNKING AND DEFENDING THE CANONS OF STATUTORY INTERPRETATION

Pages 953–55. Insert the following Note to replace the Note on Interpretive Directions in Statutes:

NOTE ON LEGISLATED CANONS OF STATUTORY INTERPRETATION

Sometimes the legislature attempts to direct the court in how to approach interpreting a particular statute. For example, a provision of the federal Racketeer Influenced and Corrupt Organizations Act (RICO), 18 U.S.C. § 1961, which contains criminal sanctions, provides that "[t]he provisions of this title shall be liberally construed to effectuate its remedial purposes." Some constitutional objections to such a provision could conceivably be raised—the most straightforward would be that it violates the separation of powers because it invades the court's power to say what the law is—but leaving that problem aside, what should a court do with it? In *Russello v. United States*, 464 U.S. 16, 26–27 (1983), the Court cited the RICO provision as well as legislative history to support a broad construction of the statute. In contrast, in *Reves v. Ernst & Young*, 507 U.S. 170, 183–84 (1993), the Court said the following about the RICO clause:

> This clause obviously seeks to ensure that Congress' intent is not frustrated by an overly narrow reading of the statute, but it is not an invitation to apply RICO to new purposes that Congress never intended. Nor does the clause help us to determine what purposes Congress had in mind. Those must be gleaned from the statute through the normal means of interpretation. The clause "only serves as an aid for resolving an ambiguity; it is not to be used to beget one."

Does this approach leave any role for the interpretive clause at all?

Congress has also adopted the Dictionary Act, which codifies a few generic canons of statutory construction, such as the rules that singular terms include the plural, and male pronouns also include females. See 1 U.S.C. § 1 et seq. All 50 states and the District of Columbia have adopted more ambitious model interpretation acts providing legislated canons to guide judicial interpretation for all statutes. Chapter 645 of the Minnesota Statutes, for example, contains the following provisions:

645.16. LEGISLATIVE INTENT CONTROLS

The object of all interpretation and construction of laws is to ascertain and effectuate the intention of the legislature. Every law shall be construed, if possible, to give effect to all its provisions.

When the words of a law in their application to an existing situation are clear and free from all ambiguity, the letter of the law shall not be disregarded under the pretext of pursuing the spirit.

When the words of a law are not explicit, the intention of the legislature may be ascertained by considering, among other matters:

(1) The occasion and necessity for the law;

(2) The circumstances under which it was enacted;

(3) The mischief to be remedied;

(4) The object to be attained;

(5) The former law, if any, including other laws upon the same or similar subjects;

(6) The consequences of a particular interpretation;

(7) The contemporaneous legislative history; and

(8) Legislative and administrative interpretations of the statute.

645.17. PRESUMPTIONS IN ASCERTAINING LEGISLATIVE INTENT

In ascertaining the intention of the legislature the courts may be guided by the following presumptions:

(1) The legislature does not intend a result that is absurd, impossible of execution, or unreasonable;

(2) The legislature intends the entire statute to be effective and certain;

(3) The legislature does not intend to violate the constitution of the United States or of this state;

(4) When a court of last resort has construed the language of a law, the legislature in subsequent laws on the same subject matter intends the same construction to be placed upon such language; and

(5) The legislature intends to favor the public interest as against any private interest.

Notice that Minnesota's legislated canons provide (1) a general theory of statutory interpretation, (2) an indication of the sources judges should consult and when they might consult them, and (3) specific presumptions of statutory meaning.

In a pathbreaking study, Jacob Scott, *Codified Canons and the Common Law of Interpretation*, 98 Geo. L.J. 341 (2010), collected and categorized the statutory canons for all 50 states and the District of Columbia. Scott then analyzed the patterns he found across the nationwide sample. Among the patterns he reported are the following:

- **Plain Meaning.** Fifteen legislatures, including that of Minnesota, have codified the plain meaning rule, but with explicit inclusion of exceptions for "absurd results" and/or "scrivener's errors" (Table 1, p. 357). Thirty-four legislatures have codified the dictionary canon and the canon that "ordinary usage" should normally be applied (Table 1). No legislature has codified *expressio unius*, and only two have codified *ejusdem generis* or *noscitur a sociis*.

- **Whole Act.** Thirty legislatures (including Minnesota's) have codified the whole act rule *and* the presumption of consistent usage of terms within a statute (Table 3, p. 368). Thirty-one have codified the rule against interpreting one provision in a way that is inconsistent with the structure of the statute (Table 3). Ten states (including Minnesota) have codified the rule against surplusage (Table 3).

- **Consistency Across Statutes.** Twenty-six states (including Minnesota) have codified the presumption that the same term should be interpreted consistently across different statutes (Table 6, p. 378). Fifteen states have codified the canon against implied repeals (Table 10, p. 397).

- **Legislative History.** Eleven states (including Minnesota) have codified the rule that legislative history "may" be considered under various circumstances; no state has legislated against consideration of legislative history (Table 7, p. 383). Like Minnesota's codification, most of these codifications require the statute to be ambiguous, but a few states (such as Texas) say legislative history can be consulted under any circumstances.

- **Constitutional Canons.** Minnesota is unusual in not codifying any of the constitutional canons. Five states have codified the avoidance canon; none has rejected it (Table 8, p. 388). Thirty-five states have codified the presumption of severability (Table 8). Twenty-four states have codified the presumption against statutory retroactivity (Table 9, p. 391).

- **Purposive Canons.** Like Minnesota, 21 other states have codified the canon that ambiguous statutes should be interpreted to carry out the legislative purpose (Table 10, p. 397). Nineteen state legislatures say that remedial statutes should be liberally construed, and 17 states say that all statutes should be liberally construed (Table 11, p. 402). Eleven states have codified the presumption that the legislature intends "reasonable" results (Table 11).

Scott argues from this exhaustive survey that there is a "common law" of canons of statutory construction—a common law to which legislatures and not just courts are contributing. He suggests that judges ought to be chary of deploying canons, such as *expressio unius* or *ejusdem generis* that legislatures have uniformly failed to embrace. If statutory interpretation is supposed to be attentive to legislative intent, as most state legislatures and courts claim, is it not relevant that legislated canons never include *expressio unius* or *ejusdem generis* and overwhelmingly endorse the absurd results exception to plain meaning and the importance of legislative purpose in resolving statutory ambiguities?

Moreover, this survey might have some traction for general theories of statutory interpretation. Scott concludes from his survey that state legislatures are not friendly to the new textualism's methodology (casebook, pp. 765–98): Although legislatures endorse the plain meaning rule, they do so with allowance for a generous absurd result exception and tend to favor consultation of legislative history and statutory purpose. Conversely, Scott suggests that the pattern of codification lends legislative, and perhaps democratic, support and legitimacy to the pragmatic approach laid out in William Eskridge, Jr. & Philip Frickey, *Statutory Interpretation as Practical Reasoning*, 42 Stan. L. Rev. 321 (1990) (casebook, pp. 830–35). How would a new textualist respond to this?

For an argument that Congress has and should exercise the authority to enact more ambitious federal rules of statutory interpretation (more like those of Minnesota and other states), see Nicholas Rosenkranz, *Federal Rules of Statutory Interpretation*, 115 Harv. L. Rev. 2085 (2002). For a critique and modification of this approach, see Adam Kiracofe, Note, *The Codified Canons of Statutory Construction: A Response and Proposal to Nicholas Rosenkranz's* Federal Rules of Statutory Interpretation, 84 B.U. L. Rev. 571 (2004). For a critique and counter-proposal suggesting that an organization like the American Law Institute formulate a restatement of statutory interpretation, see Gary O'Connor, *Restatement (First) of Statutory Interpretation*, 7 N.Y.U. J. Legis. & Pub. Pol'y 333 (2003–04).

SECTION 2.   EXTRINSIC SOURCES FOR STATUTORY INTERPRETATION

B.   LEGISLATIVE BACKGROUND (HISTORY)

2.   Committee Reports (and an Introduction to the Great Legislative History Debate)

Page 998. Add the following Case and Notes right before *Perez*:

Carr v. United States, 130 S.Ct. 2229 (2010). The Sex Offender Registration and Notification Act of 2006 (SORNA) makes it a federal crime for any person (1) who "is required to register under [SORNA]," and (2) who "travels in interstate or foreign commerce," to (3) "knowingly fai[l] to register or update a registration," 18 U.S.C. § 2250(a). Before SORNA's enactment, Thomas Carr, a registered sex offender in Alabama, relocated to Indiana without complying with Indiana's registration requirements. The federal government charged Carr with violating SORNA. After the trial court rejected his constitutional (*ex post facto*) challenge to this indictment, Carr pleaded guilty. On appeal, he argued that the statute requires that the interstate travel (as well as the failure to register or update a registration) be accomplished *after* SORNA went into effect. The government argued that only the failure to register or update needs to be after the effective date.

Reversing the Seventh Circuit, **Justice Sotomayor**'s opinion for the Court interpreted SORNA to apply only if both the travel and the failure to register/update occurred after the statute went into effect. "By its terms, the first element of § 2250(a) can only be satisfied when a person 'is required to register *under the Sex Offender Registration and Notification Act.*' § 2250(a)(1) (emphasis added)." The implication of this requirement is that SORNA is applicable to the defendant when he engages in travel and failure to register/update.

Justice Sotomayor found this reading consistent with the second requirement, that the defendant "travels" in commerce. "That § 2250 sets forth the travel requirement in the present tense ('travels') rather than in the past or present perfect ('traveled' or 'has traveled') reinforces the conclusion that pre-enactment travel falls outside the statute's compass. Consistent with normal usage, we have frequently looked to Congress' choice of verb tense to ascertain a statute's temporal reach. The Dictionary Act also ascribes significance to verb tense. It provides that, '[i]n determining the meaning of any Act of Congress, unless the context indicates otherwise[,] ... words used in the present tense include the future as well as the present.' 1 U.S.C. § 1. By implication, then, the Dictionary Act instructs that the present tense generally does not include the past. Accordingly, a statute that regulates a person who 'travels' is not readily understood to encompass a person whose only travel occurred before the statute took effect. Indeed, neither the Government nor the dissent identifies any instance in which this Court has construed a present-tense verb in a criminal law to reach pre-enactment conduct.

"The Government accepts that th[e] last element—a knowing failure to register or update a registration—must postdate SORNA's enactment. Had Congress intended pre-enactment conduct to satisfy the first two requirements of § 2250 but not the third, it presumably would have varied the verb tenses to convey this meaning. Indeed, numerous federal statutes use the past-perfect tense to describe one or more elements of a criminal offense when coverage of pre-enactment events is intended. See, e.g., 18 U.S.C. § 249(a)(2)(B)(iii) (Supp. 2010) (proscribing hate crimes in which 'the defendant employs a firearm, dangerous weapon, explosive or incendiary device, or other weapon that *has traveled* in interstate or foreign commerce' (emphasis added)); 18 U.S.C. § 922(g)(9) (2006 ed.) (proscribing firearm possession or transport by any person 'who *has been convicted*' of a felony or a misdemeanor crime of domestic violence (emphasis added). The absence of similar phrasing here provides powerful evidence that § 2250 targets only post-enactment travel.

"In a final effort to justify its position, the Government invokes one of SORNA's underlying purposes: to locate sex offenders who had failed to abide by their registration obligations. SORNA, the Government observes, was motivated at least in part by Congress' concern about these 'missing' sex offenders—a problem the House Committee on the Judiciary expressly linked to interstate travel: 'The most significant enforcement issue in the sex offender program is that over 100,000 sex offenders, or nearly one-fifth in the Nation[,] are 'missing,' meaning they have not complied with sex offender registration requirements. This typically occurs when the sex offender moves from one State to another. The goal of tracking down missing sex offenders, the Government maintains, 'is surely better served by making Section 2250 applicable to them in their new States of residence immediately than by waiting for them to travel in interstate commerce and fail to register yet again.'

"The Government's argument confuses a general goal of SORNA with the specific purpose of § 2250. Section 2250 is not a stand-alone response to the problem of missing sex offenders; it is embedded in a broader statutory scheme enacted to address the deficiencies in prior law that had enabled sex offenders to slip through the cracks. Among its many provisions, SORNA instructs States to maintain sex-offender registries that compile an array of information about sex offenders, § 16914; to make this information publicly available online, § 16918; to share the information with other jurisdictions and with the Attorney General for inclusion in a comprehensive national sex-offender registry, §§ 16919–16921; and to 'provide a criminal penalty that includes a maximum term of imprisonment that is greater than 1 year for the failure of a sex offender to comply with the requirements of this subchapter,' § 16913(e). Sex offenders, in turn, are required to 'register, and keep the registration current, in each jurisdiction where the offender resides, where the offender is an employee, and where the offender is a student,' § 16913(a), and to appear in person periodically to 'allow the jurisdiction to take a current photograph, and verify the information in each registry in which that offender is required to be registered,' § 16916. By facilitating the collection of sex-offender information and its dissemination among jurisdictions, these provisions, not § 2250, stand at the center of Congress' effort to account for missing sex offenders.

"Knowing that Congress aimed to reduce the number of noncompliant sex offenders thus tells us little about the specific policy choice Congress made in enacting § 2250. While subjecting pre-SORNA travelers to punishment under § 2250 may well be consistent with the aim of finding missing sex offenders, a contrary construction in no way frustrates that broad goal.

"None of the legislative materials the Government cites as evidence of SORNA's purpose calls this reading into question. To the contrary, the report of the House Judiciary Committee suggests not only that a prohibition on post-enactment travel is consonant with Congress' goals, but also that it is the rule Congress in fact chose to adopt. As the Government acknowledges, the bill under consideration by the Committee contained a version of § 2250 that 'would not have reached pre-enactment interstate travel.' This earlier version imposed federal criminal penalties on any person who 'receives a notice from an official that such person is required to register under [SORNA] and ... thereafter travels in interstate or foreign commerce, or enters or leaves Indian country.' H. R. Rep. No. 109–218, pt. 1, at 9. Yet this did not stop the Committee from describing its legislation as a solution to the problem of missing sex offenders. The Government identifies nothing in the legislative record to suggest that, in modifying this language during the course of the legislative process, Congress intended to alter the statute's temporal sweep."

Justice Scalia concurred in all but this last portion of the Court's opinion, discussing SORNA's legislative history. "I do not join that part because only the text Congress voted on, and not unapproved statements made or comments written during its drafting and enactment process, is an authoritative indicator of the law. But even if those pre-enactment materials were relevant, it would be unnecessary to address them here. The Court's thorough discussion of text, context, and structure demonstrates that the meaning of 18 U.S.C. § 2250(a) is plain."

Justice Alito (joined by **Justices Thomas** and **Ginsburg**) dissented. "A man convicted in State A for sexual abuse is released from custody in that State and then, after the enactment of SORNA, moves to State B and fails to register as required by State B law. Section 2250(a) makes this offender's failure to register in State B a federal crime because his interstate movement frustrates SORNA's registration requirements. Because this offender is convicted and then released from custody in State A, the State A authorities know of his presence in their State and are thus in a position to try to ensure that he remains registered. At the time of his release, they can ascertain where he intends to live, and they can make sure that he registers as required by state law. Thereafter, they can periodically check the address at which he is registered to confirm that he still resides there. And even if he moves without warning to some other address in the State, they can try to track him down. Once this offender leaves State A, however, the authorities in that State are severely limited in their ability to monitor his movements. And because the State B authorities have no notice of his entry into their State, they are at a great disadvantage in trying to enforce State B's registration law. Congress enacted § 2250(a) in order to punish and deter interstate movement that seriously undermines the enforcement of sex-offender-registration laws.

"The second case is the same as the first in all respects except that the sex offender travels from State A to State B before SORNA's enactment. In other words, the sex offender is convicted and later released in State A; prior to SORNA's enactment, he moves to State B; and then, after SORNA takes effects, he fails to register in State B, as SORNA requires.

"Is there any reason why Congress might have wanted to treat the second case any differently from the first?" Justice Alito thought not—nor did he think that the statutory text required or even supported what he considered an absurd result. The Court's argument, that § 2250(a) uses the present tense and that the "present" is the date the law was enacted, "flies in the face of the widely accepted modern legislative drafting convention that a law should *not* be read to speak as of the date of enactment. The United States Senate Legislative Drafting Manual directly addresses this point: 'A legislative provision speaks as of any date on which it is read (*rather than as of when drafted, enacted, or put into effect*).' (emphasis added). The House Manual makes the same point: 'Your draft should be a movable feast—that is, it speaks as of whatever time it is being read (*rather than as of when drafted, enacted, or put into effect*).'

"In accordance with this convention, modern legislative drafting manuals teach that, except in unusual circumstances, all laws, including penal statutes, should be written in the present tense. The Senate Manual states: '[A]lways use the present tense unless the provision addresses only the past, the future, or a sequence of events that requires use of a different tense.' Similarly, the House Manual advises: 'STAY IN THE PRESENT.—Whenever possible, use the present tense (rather than the past or future).' Numerous state legislative drafting manuals and other similar handbooks hammer home this same point." Justice Alito cited the drafting manuals used by nine different states.

"Once it is recognized that § 2250(a) should not be read as speaking as of the date when SORNA went into effect, petitioner's argument about the use of the present tense collapses. In accordance with current drafting conventions, § 2250(a) speaks, not as of the time when the law went into effect, but as of the time when the first act necessary for conviction is committed. In the case of § 2250(a), that occurs when an individual is convicted of a qualifying sex offense, for it is that act that triggers the requirement to register under SORNA." Justice Alito challenged the majority Justices to "double check" their too-confident textual analysis against the legislative history and purpose of the law.

"SORNA was a response to a dangerous gap in the then existing sex-offender-registration laws. In the years prior to SORNA's enactment, the Nation had been shocked by cases in which children had been raped and murdered by persons who, unbeknownst to their neighbors or the police, were convicted sex offenders. In response, Congress and state legislatures passed laws requiring the registration of sex offenders. Despite those efforts, by 2006 an estimated 100,000 convicted sex offenders—nearly one-fifth of the Nation's total sex-offender population—remained unregistered. The principal problem, a House Report determined, was that sex offenders commonly moved from one State to another and then failed to register in their new State of residence. In other words, interstate travel was danger-ously undermining the effectiveness of state sex-offender-registration laws.

"Interpreting § 2250(a)(2)(B) to reach only post-enactment travel severely impairs § 2250(a)'s effectiveness. As interpreted by the Court, § 2250(a) applies to a pre-SORNA sex offender only if that offender traveled in interstate commerce at some point *after* SORNA's enactment. As the examples discussed at the beginning of this opinion illustrate, however, there is no apparent reason why Congress would have wanted to impose such a requirement. To the contrary, under the Court's interpreta-tion, the many sex offenders who had managed to avoid pre-existing registration regimes, mainly by moving from one State to another before SORNA's enactment, are placed beyond the reach of the federal criminal laws. It surely better serves the enforcement of SORNA's registration requirements to apply § 2250(a) to all pre-SORNA sex offenders, regard-less of whether their interstate travel occurred before or after the stat-ute's enactment.

"The Court provides only a weak defense of the result its analysis produces. The Court suggests that enhanced information collection and sharing and state enforcement of registration laws were the sole weapons that Congress chose to wield in order to deal with those convicted sex offenders whose whereabouts were unknown when SORNA was passed. I see no basis for this conclusion. There can be no dispute that the enactment of § 2250(a) shows that Congress did not think these measures were sufficient to deal with persons who have qualifying sex-offense convictions and who move from State to State after SORNA's enactment. And in light of that congressional judgment, is there any plausible reason to think that Congress concluded that these same measures would be adequate for those with qualifying sex offense convictions who had already disappeared at the time of SORNA's enactment?"

NOTES ON THE SEX OFFENDER REGISTRATION CASE AND A NEW DIRECTION IN THE LEGISLATIVE HISTORY DEBATE

1. *The Court Continues to Discuss and Analyze Legislative History.* The Justices' debate in *Carr* provides a current snapshot of the Great Committee Report Debate within the Court, as of 2010. Since 2005, three new Justices have been confirmed (Roberts, Alito, Sotomayor), with a fourth on the way (Solicitor General Elena Kagan), and *Carr* indicates that legislative history remains alive and well at the Supreme Court level—over the continued (indeed, renewed) objections of Justice Scalia.

The dissenting Justices (Thomas, Ginsburg, and Alito), spanning the political spectrum, rely centrally on legislative history to make their case against the Court's narrow construction of SORNA. It is significant that Justice Alito's dissent does not stop after it has made its logical and textual arguments—and that Justice Sotomayor's majority opinion (for an equally heterogeneous cluster of Roberts, Stevens, Kennedy, and Breyer) responds with her own sharp-eyed analysis of the legislative history.

Justice Scalia remains alone in his objections to the admissibility of legislative history. Why does he persist? What is the purpose of his solo concurring opinions objecting to legislative history arguments in majority opinions? Jot down your thoughts, and then consider the next note.

2. *But Legislative History Is Rarely Decisive at the Supreme Court.* If the Justices continue to discuss and analyze legislative history, they do not often give it decisive effect in their opinions. Speaking for the Court (and for Justice Scalia), Justice Sotomayor's opinion says that there is a plain meaning—and the legislative history materials are discussed mainly in response to Justice Alito's dissenting opinion. But Justice Alito himself starts with a textual argument and seems to deploy legislative history mainly to confirm what he thinks the statute's plain meaning is.

Does Justice Scalia have a persuasive point, that the Court's (and, for that matter, Justice Alito's) legal analysis would not change significantly if legislative history were discarded? Because the Justices cite and discuss legislative history, lawyers in federal court cases and even advising clients must research legislative history, which generates enormous social expense. Is that expense worth the value added by legislative history? How would Justice Sotomayor respond to these concerns?

3. *A New Source of Textual Analysis: Legislative Drafting Manuals?* Justice Alito's textualist argument drawn from legislative drafting manuals caught *everyone* by surprise—the lawyers and law students working for Mr. Carr, the lawyers for the government (which had not briefed this issue), and legal academics (who had neglected this source of textual understanding). Why did his argument not garner more than three votes? Why did Justice Scalia not find it persuasive?

The element of surprise may have worked against Justice Alito. Just as the majority Justices may have been concerned with the retroactive application of a major penal statute to Mr. Carr, so they might have been worried that he should not lose the case based upon novel, unbriefed evidence of legislative practice. If this was a concern in *Carr*, however, it should *not* be a concern in future cases. The word is now out, that both the House and the Senate have drafting manuals that provide potentially important insights into how legislators understand, as a conventional matter, the textualist rules of the game. Moreover, both manuals are available on-line and so are easily available to lawyers and judges. The House Manual has long been on-line, at http://www.thecapitol.net/Research/images/HOLC.Manual.on.Drafting.Style. 1995.pdf (viewed June 26, 2010). Although not previously on-line, the Senate Manual is now available at http://www.law.yale.edu/faculty/legislative materials.htm (viewed June 26, 2010).

An important student comment argues that textualists ought to pay attention to legislative drafting manuals. See Franklin Ard, Comment, *Legislative Drafting Manuals as a Guide to Statutory Interpretation*, 120 Yale L.J. ___ (forthcoming 2010). Ard points out that one critique of the new textualism is that it represents a judicial bait-and-switch game on Congress: Legislators enact statutes under conventional assumptions that text-loving judges later ignore and even thwart. When the legislative assumptions are well-documented rules for drafting statutory *texts*, then the new textualism seems theoretically mistaken, and the good faith of its users might be questioned. Should Justice Scalia incorporate legislative drafting manuals in his arsenal now? (Ard believes that drafting manuals are not the textualist treasure trove that dictionaries are, but he does claim that new textualists need to consider them as well.)

If *Carr* stimulates a new cottage industry surveying legislative drafting manuals, might that not render textualist analysis even more complicated? The more sources textualists draw into their net, the more judges will be tempted to look out over the crowd and pick out their friends. Cf. Adrian Vermeule, *Judging Under Uncertainty* (2006) (worrying that the new textualism is already subject to this problem).

Page 998. Replace the Note on the Norplant Case etc. with the following Note:

Note on the Norplant Case and State Court Reliance on Committee and Other Legislative Reports

The Norplant Case is an unusually apt one for consideration of legislative history, as the statute itself contained a reference to the committee report.[a] Moreover, **New Jersey** is one of about a dozen states that have regular reports from standing committees to accompany legislation, and it is one of eight states to make committee reports for recent legislation available on-line. See Brian Barnes, "The Transformation of State Statutory Interpretation," at

---

a. Compare *Landgraf v. USI Film Products* (casebook, pp. 672–85), in which the statute contained a provision limiting judicial reference to legislative history. Should a strict textualist honor a statutory text requiring judges to consult legislative history? Compare Jonathan Siegel, *The Use of Legislative History in a System of Separated Powers*, 53 Vand. L. Rev. 1457 (2000) (statutory incorporation by reference of legislative history removes separation-of-powers objection) with John Manning, *Putting Legislative History to a Vote: A Response to Professor Siegel*, 53 Vand. L. Rev. 1529 (2000) (taking contrary position).

7 (Yale Law School Seminar Paper, May 4, 2010). Traditionally, New Jersey state judges are among the most willing to rely on legislative history to construe statutes; judges in that state sometimes consider committee reports whether or not the statute's text is ambiguous. See, *e.g.*, *State v. Fleischman*, 917 A.2d 722, 730 n.4 (N.J. 2007) (committee report and whole act creating textual ambiguity, triggering rule of lenity); *State v. Hoffman*, 695 A.2d 236 (N.J. 1997); *Wingate v. Estate of Ryan*, 693 A.2d 457 (N.J. 1997); N.J. Stat. § 40:41A–1 et seq. But compare *New Jersey Civ. Serv. Ass'n v. State*, 443 A.2d 1070 (N.J. 1982) (committee reports may not trump clear words of statute).

As in other states, the methodological lay-of-the-land in New Jersey is subject to challenge and possible change; Governor Chris Christie, elected in 2009, theoretically will have a chance to appoint four new justices, a majority of the court, and has vowed to appoint strict textualists in the mold of Justice Scalia.[b] Should Governor Christie cite the Norplant Case as an example of contextualist interpretation gone awry? Or should he consider Justice Pollock's dissent (relying on the committee report and other legislative materials) to be the best approach to the issues in the Norplant Case?

For recent examples of state appellate courts' reliance on committee reports, see *People v. Gonzalez*, 184 P.3d 702 (**California** 2008); *Aiken v. United States*, 956 A.2d 33, 43–44 (**District of Columbia** 2008); *State v. Woodfall*, 206 P.3d 841, 847–50 (**Hawaii** 2009); *State v. Dohlman*, 725 N.W.2d 428, 432 (**Iowa** 2006); *Risdall v. Brown–Wilbert, Inc.*, 753 N.W.2d 723, 730 & n.6 (**Minnesota** 2008); *State v. Neesley*, 239 S.W.3d 780, 785–86 (**Texas** Crim. App. 2007).

In many other states a "bill report" is prepared by the committee staff after a bill is voted out of committee, but it is not necessarily reviewed by the committee or even its chair. The bill report typically contains a background statement, a summary of the bill's provisions, changes made by the committee, a list of the proponents and opponents who testified before the committee, and the pro and con arguments. Courts will sometimes discount such sources. In *Gates v. Jensen*, 595 P.2d 919 (**Washington** 1979), for example, the court failed to mention a bill report that explained the ambit of a statutory override of the Court's prior decisions imposing a rather strict standard of care in medical malpractice actions. Dissenting justices argued from the bill report that the override went further than the majority was willing to take it. The current trend among the states is to consider bill reports as weak but admissible evidence of legislative intent. The Supreme Court of **Florida** has deemed bill reports "one touchstone of the legislative will." *White v. State*, 714 So.2d 440, 443 n.5 (1998), also *State v. Jefferson*, 758 So.2d 661, 665–66 (**Florida** 2000); accord, *People v. Ramirez*, 201 P.3d 466, 470 (**California** 2009) and *In re Derrick B.*, 139 P.3d 485 (**California** 2006); *Kramer v. Liberty Prop. Trust*, 968 A.2d 120 (**Maryland** 2009); *Fournier v. Elliott*, 966 A.2d 410 (**Maine** 2009); *Kern v. Blethen–Coluni*, 612 N.W.2d 838 (**Michigan** App. 2000); *Krupa v. State*, 2009 WL 1163430 (**Texas** Crim. App. 4/29/2009);

---

b. We learned this bit of political intelligence, as well as confirmation of New Jersey's highly contextual approach to statutory interpretation, from Adam Yoffie, "Statutory Interpretation at the State Level: A Case Study of the New Jersey Supreme Court, 2000–2010" (Yale Law School, May 28, 2010).

Cosmopolitan Engr'g Group, Inc. v. Ondeo Degremont, Inc., 149 P.3d 666, 672–73 (**Washington** 2006).

In **New York**, the governor's staff compiles a "bill jacket" (the New York term) to assist the governor in her or his decision whether to veto a bill the legislature has passed. Containing analyses from legislative sponsors as well as interested agencies and private parties, bill jackets are often treasure troves of legislative background materials and legal arguments. Similar reports, called "governor's bills files," can be found in public archives for California, Massachusetts, Oregon, Utah, Washington, and perhaps other states. *E.g., Ramirez,* 201 P.3d at 471–72 (relying on sponsor's letter to file compiled for governor in **California**).

In addition to committee reports and bill reports, state legislative history can include a number of other reports compiled by official sources before statutes are enacted. In her dissenting opinion in *State ex rel. Kalal v. Circuit Ct., Dane Cnty.,* 681 N.W.2d 110, 125–26 (**Wisconsin** 2004), Chief Justice Shirley Abrahamson listed other sources her court had traditionally considered, including not just legislative committee reports, but also legislative reference bureau drafting files and prefatory notes for bills, governor's study commission reports, judicial council notes, joint legislative council notes, and governor's veto messages. Wisconsin's Supreme Court still routinely relies on such materials. *E.g., State v. Duchow,* 749 N.W.2d 913 (Wis. 2008) (legislative reference bureau's drafting file); *State v. Grunke,* 738 N.W.2d 137, 142 (Wis. 2007) (same). See also *Price v. Thomas Built Buses, Inc.,* 260 S.W.3d 300, 305–06 (**Arkansas** 2007) (resolving ambiguity by reference to legislative council report); *Jones v. Lodge,* 177 P.3d 232, 240–43 (**California** 2008) (relying on legislative counsel's digest summarizing bills, as well as committee report and agency bill analysis); *People v. Garson,* 848 N.E.2d 1264 (**New York** 2006) (commission staff notes relied on); *McKinney v. Richetelli,* 586 S.E.2d 258, 263 (**North Carolina** 2003) (report of general statutes commission).

In at least one state, there has been serious debate as to what kinds of legislative materials might be admissible. An important decision is *People v. Gardner,* 753 N.W.2d 78, 89 (**Michigan** 2008), where a divided Michigan Supreme Court ruled that legislative materials could only be considered when the statute is ambiguous *and* that only certain legislative materials should be admissible. *Admissible* materials included the statutory history and evidence of proposals rejected by one chamber or the other. *Inadmissible* materials, even when the statute is ambiguous, included committee reports, staff analyses of bills, and floor speeches by sponsors and other legislators. In 2008, the textualist chief justice was turned out of office by the voters, and the Michigan Supreme Court may not remain committed to such a stingy view in subsequent cases.

Consideration of committee and bill reports is hardly a monopoly of large-population states. Practices similar to those in the previous paragraphs can be found in **Alaska**, see, e.g., *Gossman v. Greatland Directional Drilling, Inc.,* 973 P.2d 93 (Alaska 1999); **Arizona**, see, e.g., *O'Malley Lumber Co. v. Riley,* 613 P.2d 629 (Ariz. App. 1980); **Connecticut**, see, e.g., *Burke v. Fleet Nat'l*

Bank, 742 A.2d 293 (Conn. 1999); *State v. Ledbetter*, 692 A.2d 713 (Conn. 1997); **Oregon**, see, e.g., *State v. Laemoa*, 533 P.2d 370 (Or. App. 1975).

Some states have no high-court authorization for considering committee reports but may be open to the practice in cases yet to be decided. Although its judges will discuss "statutory history" (the formal evolution of the statute, as amended over time), appellate courts in **Missouri, Virginia**, and **Georgia** do not cite to legislative history. *E.g.*, *Sikes v. State*, 485 S.E.2d 206, 211 (Ga. 1997); *State v. Premium Standard Farms, Inc.*, 100 S.W.3d 157 (Mo. App. 2003). Many smaller states have no readily available legislative history, and there are too few reported decisions to discern a hard-and-fast rule for lawyer use of legislative history. *E.g.*, **Rhode Island**, *Such v. State,* 950 A.2d 1150, 1158–59 (2008); **Wyoming**, *Moncrief v. Harvey*, 816 P.2d 97, 111–12 (1991) (Urbigkit, J., dissenting). Finally, legislative history at the state level is more accessible than it was a generation ago. See William Manz, *Guide to State Legislative and Administrative Materials* (7th ed. 2008); Barnes, "Transformation of State Statutory Interpretation" (documenting how every category of legislative history is much more widely available in 2010 than it was in 1980, and much of the recent materials are available on-line). Indeed, judges are sometimes even encouraging counsel to research it. In *Dillehey v. State*, 815 S.W.2d 623 (**Texas** Crim. App. 1991), the appeals court not only relied on legislative history but, in an appendix to the court's opinion, provided counsel in future cases with a roadmap for researching legislative history in Texas. Increasingly, state legislative history is on-line. Some state supreme courts provide guides to researching legislative history on their websites.[c]

3.   Statements by Sponsors or Drafters of Legislation

Page 1014. Insert the following Note right before *Kosak*:

NOTE ON STATE COURT RELIANCE ON SPONSOR'S STATEMENTS

Like the U.K. House of Lords, and unlike the U.S. Supreme Court, state supreme courts in this country rely perhaps more heavily on the statements of legislative sponsors than on committee or bill reports as the sources for illumination about legislative expectations. A large majority of states make available to the public transcripts of legislative floor debates and of committee hearings. See Brian Barnes, "The Transformation of State Statutory Interpretation," at 10–11 (Yale Law School Seminar Paper, May 4, 2010) (33 states offer transcripts or tapes of current legislative floor debates, with 17 offering them on-line as of 2010); *id.* at 12–13 (37 states offer transcripts or tapes of current committee hearings, with 16 offering them on-line as of 2010). Much of the floor debate consists of statements by the sponsor or floor manager presenting the case for the proposed legislation, responding to objections made by opponents, and answering questions posed by colleagues.

Committee chairs (who are usually later the floor managers) play a large role in committee hearings, making speeches, questioning witnesses, and explaining proposed legislation. Because the sponsor/floor manager is usually

---

c. See, e.g., the Washington Supreme Court's website, www.courts.wa.gov/library/legis.cfm (viewed June 20, 2010).

the most knowledgeable legislator on topics relating to the proposed legislation and usually represents the coalition pushing for the legislation, his or her
statements are much more probative than those of other legislators. Recall,
for example, the Oregon Court of Appeals decision in *PGE* (Chapter 7, this
Supplement), where the dissenting judges relied on the explanation by the
committee chair.

For examples of recent state supreme court decisions relying on statements by legislative sponsors or floor managers, see *State v. Batts,* 195 P.3d
144, 151–52 (**Alaska** 2008) (sponsor's explanation critical evidence of statutory meaning); *Carter v. Calif. Dep't of Veterans Affairs,* 135 P.3d 637, 646–47
(**California** 2006) (treating sponsor's memo as authoritative but finding that
it does not answer the issue before the court); *CLPF–Parkridge One, L.P. v.
Harwell Invs., Inc.,* 105 P.3d 658, 664–65 (**Colorado** 2005) (relying entirely
on legislative history to interpret law); *People v. Collins,* 824 N.E.2d 262, 267
(**Illinois** 2005); *State v. Allen,* 708 N.W.2d 361, 366–67 (**Iowa** 2006); *Rural
Water Dist. #2 v. City of Louisburg,* 207 P.3d 1055 (**Kansas** 2009) (post-
enactment letter from sponsor invoked to support plain meaning); *Kentucky
Pub. Serv. Comm'n v. Commonwealth ex rel. Stumbo,* 2008 WL 4822263
(**Kentucky** App. 2008); *Stockman Bank of Mont. v. Mon–Kota, Inc.,* 180 P.3d
1125 (**Montana** 2008); *Chanos v. Nev. Tax Comm'n,* 181 P.3d 675, 680 &
n.17 (**Nevada** 2008); *State v. Mayes,* 186 P.3d 293, 297–98 (**Oregon** App.
2008) (relying on evidence from drafter as well as sponsor); *Stewart Title
Guar. Co. v. State Tax Assessor,* 963 A.2d 169, 178–79 (**Maine** 2009) (ambiguity resolved by reference to statutory history as explained by sponsor);
Kramer v. Liberty Prop. Trust, 968 A.2d 120 (**Maryland** 2009) (sponsor's
statement confirms plain meaning); *Commonwealth v. Ahlborn,* 626 A.2d 1265
(**Pennsylvania** 1993); *Lawrence County Educ. Ass'n v. Lawrence County Bd.
of Educ.,* 244 S.W.3d 302, 312 (**Tennessee** 2007); *Dep't of Corr. v. Human
Rights Comm'n,* 917 A.2d 451, 453 (**Vermont** 2006).

Like the U.S. Supreme Court, state supreme courts will not credit stray
statements by legislators who are probably not speaking for the enacting
coalition. See, *e.g., Wright v. Home Depot U.S.A., Inc.,* 142 P.3d 265, 275 n.8
(**Hawaii** 2006). Likewise, state supreme courts (like federal courts) will not
credit post-hoc affidavits by the sponsors or floor managers of enacted bills,
because the post-hoc nature of such evidence deprives it of reliability. Efforts
to invoke after-the-fact legislator affidavits often occur (and are usually
rebuffed) in states where there is not (at the time) much publicly available
legislative material. See, *e.g., Tomei v. Sharp,* 902 A.2d 757, 769 n.41
(**Delaware** Super. 2006); *Utility Center, Inc. v. City of Fort Wayne,* 868
N.E.2d 453, 459–60 (**Indiana** 2007); *DIRECTV, Inc. v. Levin,* 907 N.E.2d
1242, 1253 (**Ohio** App. 2009); *LaPlante v. Honda N. Am., Inc.,* 697 A.2d 625,
628–29 (**Rhode Island** 1997); **South Carolina,** *Kennedy v. S.C. Ret. Sys.,*
549 S.E.2d 243, 247 & n.4, 250–51 (2001); *Phillips v. Larry's Drive–In
Pharmacy, Inc.,* 647 S.E.2d 920, 924–26 (**West Virginia** 2007).

CHAPTER 9

IMPLEMENTATION AND INTERPRETATION OF STATUTES IN THE ADMINISTRATIVE STATE

■ ■ ■

SECTION 2. CONGRESSIONAL INFLUENCE OVER STATUTORY IMPLEMENTATION

F. JUDICIAL REVIEW OF AGENCY RULES AND ORDERS

Page 1185. Insert the following Case and Notes at the end of Section 2:

FCC v. Fox Television Stations, Inc., 129 S.Ct. 1800 (2009). Federal law prohibits the broadcasting of "any ... indecent ... language," 18 U.S.C. § 1464, which includes expletives referring to sexual or excretory activity or organs, see *FCC v. Pacifica Foundation,* 438 U.S. 726 (1978). For many years, the FCC followed an announced regulatory approach that banned sexual or excretory "expletives" only if their use was "deliberate and repetitive"; mere "fleeting" expletives would generally be allowed. Even as the FCC expanded its indecency standard to encompass ever more words and phrases, it preserved this approach—until a 2006 FCC ruling against Fox. In that ruling, the FCC rejected its longstanding distinction between "expletive" and "literal" uses of terms like "fuck" as "artificial." Also, the FCC ended its tolerance for "fleeting" expletives, finding that they have the power to offend parents and children, and that permitting them gives broadcasters too much freedom to be offensive.

Invoking the Supreme Court's decision in *State Farm* (casebook, pp. 1176–83), the Second Circuit overturned the agency's order against Fox on the ground that the FCC had not adequately explained why it was jettisoning its longstanding rule The Supreme Court reversed, in an opinion by **Justice Scalia**. "We find no basis in the Administrative Procedure Act or in our opinions for a requirement that all agency [action that changes prior policy] be subjected to more searching review. The Act mentions no such heightened standard. And our opinion in *State Farm* neither held nor implied that every agency action representing a policy change must be justified by reasons more substantial than those required to adopt a policy in the first instance. That case, which involved the rescission of a prior regulation, said only that such action requires 'a reasoned analysis for the change beyond that which may be required when an agency *does not act* in the first instance.' ([E]mphasis added). Treating failures to act and rescissions of prior action differently for purposes of the standard of review makes good sense, and has basis in the text of the [APA], which likewise treats the two separately. It instructs a reviewing court to 'compel agency action unlawfully withheld or unreasonably delayed,' 5 U.S.C. § 706(1), and to 'hold unlawful and set aside agency action, findings, and conclusions found to be [among other things] … arbitrary [or] capricious,' § 706(2)(A). The statute makes no distinction, however, between initial agency action and subsequent agency action undoing or revising that action. (1996).

"To be sure, the requirement that an agency provide reasoned explanation for its action would ordinarily demand that it display awareness that it *is* changing position. An agency may not, for example, depart from a prior policy *sub silentio* or simply disregard rules that are still on the books. And of course the agency must show that there are good reasons for the new policy. But it need not demonstrate to a court's satisfaction that the reasons for the new policy are *better* than the reasons for the old one; it suffices that the new policy is permissible under the statute, that there are good reasons for it, and that the agency *believes* it to be better, which the conscious change of course adequately indicates. This means that the agency need not always provide a more detailed justification than what would suffice for a new policy created on a blank slate. Sometimes it must—when, for example, its new policy rests upon factual findings that contradict those which underlay its prior policy; or when its prior policy has engendered serious reliance interests that must be taken into account. It would be arbitrary or capricious to ignore such matters. In such cases it is not that further justification is demanded by the mere fact of policy change; but that a reasoned explanation is needed for disregarding facts and circumstances that underlay or were engendered by the prior policy."

Under this understanding of the law, Justice Scalia ruled that the FCC's order was not "arbitrary and capricious." The FCC had "forthrightly acknowledged" that it was creating new policy and repudiating inconsistent prior actions taken by the Commission and staff. Also, the FCC's reasons for its decision were "entirely rational." It was reasonable for the FCC to conclude that the literal-expletive distinction was nonsensical given that both kinds of uses could cause offense and subject children to a harmful "first blow" of indecency; given technological advances, it was reasonable for the FCC to expect broadcasters to "bleep out" even fleeting expletives.

Justice Kennedy joined Justice Scalia's opinion as to all of the foregoing matters but issued a concurring opinion that nonetheless took a somewhat different approach than Justice Scalia's opinion, which needed Kennedy's vote to represent a majority. "The question whether a change in policy requires an agency to provide a more-reasoned explanation than when the original policy was first announced is not susceptible, in my view, to an answer that applies in all cases. * * *

"The question in each case is whether the agency's reasons for the change, when viewed in light of the data available to it, and when informed by the experience and expertise of the agency, suffice to demonstrate that the new policy rests upon principles that are rational, neutral, and in accord with the agency's proper understanding of its authority. * * *

"Where there is a policy change the record may be much more developed because the agency based its prior policy on factual findings. In that instance, an agency's decision to change course may be arbitrary and capricious if the agency ignores or countermands its earlier factual findings without reasoned explanation for doing so. An agency cannot simply disregard contrary or inconvenient factual determinations that it made in the past, any more than it can ignore inconvenient facts when it writes on a blank slate." This is the lesson Justice Kennedy drew from *State Farm*. "The present case does not raise the concerns addressed in *State Farm*" because the FCC had based its prior policy not on factual findings, but on its interpretation of the Court's *Pacifica* ruling, and had given appropriate reasons for changing its policy.

Justice Stevens dissented in an opinion emphasizing the FCC's status as an independent agency, which, he believed, should be relatively free from political influence. "The FCC, like all agencies, may revise its regulations from time to time, just as Congress amends its statutes as circumstances warrant. But the FCC is constrained by its congressional mandate. There should be a strong presumption that the FCC's initial views, reflecting the informed judgment of independent commissioners with expertise in the regulated area, also reflect the views of the Congress that delegated the Commission authority to flesh out details not fully defined in the enacting statute. The rules adopted after *Pacifica* have been in effect for decades and have not proved unworkable in the intervening years. * * * [B]roadcasters have a substantial interest in regulatory stability; the threat of crippling financial penalties looms large over these entities. The FCC's shifting and impermissibly vague indecency policy only imperils these broadcasters and muddles the regulatory landscape. It therefore makes eminent sense to require the Commission to justify why its prior policy is no longer sound before allowing it to change course. The FCC's congressional charter, the Administrative Procedure Act, § 706(2)(A) (instructing courts to 'hold unlawful and set aside ... arbitrary [or] capricious' agency action), and the rule of law all favor stability over administrative whim." (1996).

Justice Breyer (joined by **Justices Stevens**, **Souter**, and **Ginsburg**) dissented. He started with the premise that, as an independent agency, the FCC was relatively insulated from political oversight. "That insulation helps to secure important governmental objectives, such as the constitutionally related objective of maintaining broadcast regulation that does not bend too readily before the political winds. But that agency's comparative freedom from ballot-box control makes it all the more important that courts review its decisionmaking to assure compliance with applicable provisions of the law—including law requiring that major policy decisions be based upon articulable reasons." Additionally, the agency must act consistently, and when it changes its own rules the agency must focus on the fact of change and explain the basis for that change.

"To explain a change requires more than setting forth reasons why the new policy is a good one. It also requires the agency to answer the question, 'Why did you change?' And a rational answer to this question typically requires a more complete explanation than would prove satisfactory were change itself not at issue." *State Farm* "requires the agency here to focus upon the reasons that led the agency to adopt the initial policy, and to explain why it now comes to a new judgment.

"I recognize that *sometimes* the ultimate explanation for a change may have to be, 'We now weigh the relevant considerations differently.' But at other times, an agency can and should say more. Where, for example, the agency rested its previous policy on particular factual findings; or where an agency rested its prior policy on its view of the governing law; or where an agency rested its previous policy on, say, a special need to coordinate with another agency, one would normally expect the agency to focus upon those earlier views of fact, of law, or of policy and explain why they are no longer controlling. Regardless, to say that the agency here must answer the question 'why change' is not to require the agency to provide a justification that is '*better* than the reasons for the old [policy].' It is only to recognize the obvious fact that *change* is sometimes (not always) a relevant background feature that sometimes (not always) requires focus (upon prior justifications) and explanation lest the adoption of the new policy (in that circumstance) be 'arbitrary, capricious, an abuse of discretion.' "

Like the Second Circuit, Justice Breyer concluded that the FCC's decision violated the *State Farm* requirement that an agency making a policy change "consider . . . important aspect[s] of the problem." In particular, he faulted the FCC for failing adequately to consider its new policy's First Amendment implications and potential impact on local broadcasters, many of whom might not be able to afford the technology necessary to "bleep out" fleeting expletives. Justice Breyer dismissed as inadequate the various reasons the FCC had adduced for its policy change—in particular, the claim that the literal-expletive distinction was nonsensical and the claim that the new policy better protects children against "the first blow" of broadcast indecency. Neither of these claims, Justice Breyer argued, could justify the FCC's policy *change* since both claims remained conclusory, failing to address the rationales underlying the prior policy.

NOTES ON WHEN AGENCY POLICY SHIFTS ARE "ARBITRARY": STATE FARM v. FOX TELEVISION

State Farm can be read as trying to strike a balance between two kinds of risks attending judicial review of agency policy changes. On the one hand, if courts are too deferential, there is the "yo-yo" risk that agency policies will fluctuate too frequently. On the other hand, if courts are too scrutinizing, there is the "ossification" risk that agencies will become too loath to change their policies. While the *State Farm* Court and the *Fox* dissenters seem to be more troubled by the yo-yo risk than the ossification risk, the *Fox* Court seems to have the opposite concern. Is *Fox* therefore inconsistent with *State Farm*? If so, can the inconsistency be justified?

1. *Independent Versus Executive Agencies?* The agency in *State Farm* was an executive department directly accountable to the President, while the agency in *Fox* was an independent agency. The dissenters, of course, argue that, because of the relative insulation of independent agencies from political pressures, policy changes made by independent agencies should be subject to *more* stringent judicial scrutiny than those made by executive agencies and, consequently, that *State Farm* applies a fortiori to *Fox*. But might the opposite be true? Might the relative insulation of independent agencies from political pressures lead one to expect their decisions to be generally *more* reasoned than the decisions of executive agencies and thus to merit *more* deference from courts?

Writing for a plurality of Justices (Part III.E of his opinion, which Justice Kennedy did not join), Justice Scalia argues that independent agencies like the FCC are subject to significant political pressures exerted by Congress through its oversight authority. Thus, "independent" agencies are not necessarily free from politics; the political pressure just comes from different branches of government. (In fact, Justice Scalia argues that the FCC's new policy in *Fox Television* was a direct consequence of congressional complaints that families were being subjected to inappropriate language during prime-time television.) But once again, might the opposite be true? Might the political accountability of independent agencies lead one to expect their decisions to be *as poorly* reasoned as those of executive agencies and thus to merit *as much* scrutiny from courts?

Should APA judicial review distinguish between the kind of agency promulgating the evolving policy that is being reviewed?

2. *Facts Versus Norms.* Rather than trying to distinguish *State Farm* and *Fox* based on the different kinds of *agencies* involved in each, one might try to distinguish them based on the different kinds of *policies* involved in each: Whereas the policy in *State Farm* seemed to be based on a relatively technical cost-benefit analysis, the policy in *Fox* seemed to be based more on a social or moral judgment.

This difference might help to explain Justice Scalia's observation about the difficulty of obtaining data about the harmfulness of fleeting expletives in broadcasts and the comparative ease of obtaining data about the benefits of passive restraints in automobiles. Perhaps the FCC's policy change rested on the judgment that, whatever the tangible harm caused by fleeting expletives, it was simply *wrong* or *immoral* to expose the public—and especially children—to such indecency. If this was in fact the nature of the FCC's judgment, should courts be more or less willing to defer to it than they would be to defer to a more technical cost-benefit analysis?

Note also that the moral judgment represented in *Fox* raises important First Amendment concerns not present in the cost-benefit judgment represented in *State Farm*: Isn't a "fleeting expletive" a classic example of free expression? Cf. *Cohen v. California*, 403 U.S. 15 (1971) (invalidating state censorship of a young man with "Fuck the Draft" on his jacket). As *Pacifica* held, Congress has greater leeway to regulate indecent speech on the radio and television than in newspapers and the print media—but the regulatory authority is not unlimited. Shouldn't there be more specific guidance from Congress as to such important matters—or is Justice Scalia probably right, that Congress was behind the FCC's tighter rule? (1996).

3. *The Difference Process Might Make?* Should process distinguish *State Farm* from *Fox Television*? The obvious process difference is that the former was a rulemaking proceeding, while the latter was an agency adjudication— but that difference might just as easily cut the other way. That is, a shift in agency policy might be more legitimate in the kind of rulemaking that *State Farm* overturned than in the adjudication that *Fox Television* sanctioned. In notice-and-comment rulemaking, for example, a greater variety of interests will submit formal analyses, and the agency must consider them—in contrast to adjudication, where the agency must only respond to the parties' presentations.

Another possible process distinction is that the DOT's auto safety policy had been a political football through several administrations, and the *State Farm* Court might have felt that the agency needed to buckle down and take its law work more seriously. In contrast, perhaps, the FCC's policy was more stable over several administrations. Although the FCC was moving policy toward greater regulation in *Fox Television*, it was making a small step (expanding the longstanding policy to include "fleeting" expletives), and a step that was arguably justified by proliferation of fleeting expletives during prime time (when more children are watching TV) and by technology allowing networks to bleep out fleeting expletives.

Are any of these distinctions persuasive—or is *Fox Television* simply a precedent-narrowing reading of *State Farm*? Should *State Farm* be reframed, or even overruled?

SECTION 3. JUDICIAL DEFERENCE TO AGENCY INTERPRETATIONS

B. IMPORTANT *CHEVRON* ISSUES

2. Does the Agency Have Broader Freedom to Interpret Its Own Rules?

Page 1245. Insert the following Case and Notes at the end of Subpart 2:

COEUR ALASKA, INC. v. SOUTHEAST ALASKA CONSERVATION COUNCIL

United States Supreme Court, 2009
___ U.S. ___, 129 S.Ct. 2458, 174 L.Ed.2d 193

JUSTICE KENNEDY delivered the opinion of the Court.

[Coeur Alaska proposed to reopen a defunct gold mine in Alaska. To extract the gold, it planned to use a technique known as "froth flotation" in which crushed rock from the mine would be churned in tanks of chemical-laden, frothing water. Gold-bearing minerals would float to the surface, where they would be skimmed off. Coeur Alaska sought permission to discharge the remaining mixture of crushed rock and water, known as slurry, into Lower Slate Lake, a navigable waterway of the United States subject to the Clean Water Act (CWA or Act). The discharge would eventually raise the lakebed to the current surface, significantly expanding the lake's area.

[Respondents, a coalition of three environmental groups known as SEACC, challenged the decision of the Army Corps of Engineers to grant Coeur Alaska a permit for the discharge on two grounds: (1) that only the EPA, not the Corps, had authority under the CWA to grant the permit and (2) that, even if the Corps had permitting authority, it could not grant the permit without violating an EPA regulation known as a "new source performance standard," promulgated under the CWA.]

[II.A] Section 402 gives the EPA authority to issue "permit[s] for the discharge of any pollutant," with one important exception: The EPA may not issue permits for fill material that fall under the Corps' § 404 permitting authority. Section 402(a) states:

"Except as provided in ... [CWA § 404, 33 U.S.C. § 1344], the Administrator may ... issue a permit for the discharge of any pollutant, ... notwithstanding [CWA § 301(a), 33 U.S.C. § 1311(a)], upon condition that such discharge will meet either (A) all applicable requirements under [CWA § 301, 33 U.S.C. § 1311(a), and other enumerated provisions], or (B) prior to the taking of necessary implementing actions relating to all such requirements, such conditions as the Administrator determines are necessary to carry out the provisions of this chapter." 33 U.S.C. § 1342(a)(1) (emphasis added). * * *

The Act is best understood to provide that if the Corps has authority to issue a permit for a discharge under § 404, then the EPA lacks authority to do so under § 402.

Even if there were ambiguity on this point, the EPA's own regulations would resolve it. Those regulations provide that "[d]ischarges of dredged or fill material into waters of the United States which are regulated under section 404 of CWA" "do not require [§ 402] permits" from the EPA. 40 CFR § 122.3. * * * Before us, the EPA confirms this reading of the regulation. Brief for Federal Respondents 27. The agency's interpretation is not "plainly erroneous or inconsistent with the regulation"; and so we accept it as correct. *Auer* [casebook, p. 1242].

The question whether the EPA is the proper agency to regulate the slurry discharge thus depends on whether the Corps of Engineers has authority to do so. If the Corps has authority to issue a permit, then the EPA may not do so. We turn to the Corps' authority under § 404.

[II.B] Section 404(a) gives the Corps power to "issue permits ... for the discharge of dredged or fill material." 33 U.S.C. § 1344(a). As all parties concede, the slurry meets the definition of fill material agreed upon by the agencies in a joint regulation promulgated in 2002. That regulation defines "fill material" to mean any "material [that] has the effect of ... [c]hanging the bottom elevation" of water—a definition that includes "slurry, or tailings or similar mining-related materials." 40 CFR § 232.2. * * *

Rather than challenge the agencies' decision to define the slurry as fill, SEACC instead contends that § 404 contains an implicit exception. According to SEACC, § 404 does not authorize the Corps to permit a discharge of fill material if that material is subject to an EPA new source performance standard.

But § 404's text does not limit its grant of power in this way. Instead, § 404 refers to all "fill material" without qualification. Nor do the EPA regulations support SEACC's reading of § 404. The EPA has enacted guidelines, pursuant to § 404(b), to guide the Corps permitting decision. 40 CFR pt. 230. Those guidelines do not strip the Corps of power to issue permits for fill in cases where the fill is also subject to an EPA new source performance standard. * * *

[III] A second question remains: In issuing the permit did the Corps act in violation of a statutory mandate so that the issuance was "not in accordance with law"? 5 U.S.C. § 706(2)(A). SEACC contends that the slurry discharge will violate the EPA's new source performance standard and that the Corps permit is made "unlawful" by CWA § 306(e). Petitioners and the agencies argue that the permit is lawful because the EPA performance standard, and § 306(e), do not apply to fill material regulated by the Corps. In order to determine whether the Corps permit is lawful we must answer the question: Do EPA performance standards, and § 306(e), apply to discharges of fill material? * * *

[III.A]   As for the statutory argument, SEACC claims the CWA § 404 permit is unlawful because § 306(e) forbids the slurry discharge. Petitioners and the federal agencies, in contrast, contend that § 306(e) does not apply to the slurry discharge.

(1) To address SEACC's statutory argument, it is necessary to review the EPA's responsibilities under the CWA. As noted, § 306 empowers the EPA to regulate the froth-flotation gold mining industry. Pursuant to this authority, EPA promulgated the new source performance standard relied upon by SEACC. The standard is stringent. If it were to apply here, it would allow "no discharge of process wastewater" from the mine. 40 CFR § 440.104(b)(1).

The term "process wastewater" includes solid waste. So the regulation forbids not only pollutants that dissolve in water but also solid pollutants suspended in water—what the agency terms "total suspended solids," or TSS. See § 440.104(a) (limiting the amount of TSS from other kinds of mines) * * *.

When the performance standard applies to a point source, § 306(e) makes it "unlawful" for that point source to violate it: "[I]t shall be unlawful for any owner or operator of any new source to operate such source in violation of any standard of performance applicable to such source." CWA § 306(e), 33 U.S.C. § 1316(e).

SEACC argues that this provision, § 306(e), forbids the mine from discharging slurry into Lower Slate Lake. SEACC contends the new source performance standard is, in the words of § 306(e), "applicable to" the mine. * * *

(2) For their part, the State of Alaska and the federal agencies claim that the Act is unambiguous in the opposite direction. They rely on § 404 of the Act. As explained above, that section authorizes the Corps of Engineers to determine whether to issue a permit allowing the discharge of the slurry. Petitioners and the agencies argue that § 404 grants the Corps authority to do so without regard to the EPA's new source performance standard or the § 306(e) prohibition discussed above.

Petitioners and the agencies make two statutory arguments based on § 404's silence in regard to § 306. First, they note that nothing in § 404 requires the Corps to consider the EPA's new source performance standard or the § 306(e) prohibition. That silence advances the argument that § 404's grant of authority to "issue permits" contradicts § 306(e)'s declaration that discharges in violation of new source performance standards are "unlawful."

Second, petitioners and the agencies point to § 404(p), which protects § 404 permitees from enforcement actions by the EPA or private citizens:

"Compliance with a permit issued pursuant to this section ... shall be deemed compliance, for purposes of sections 1319 [CWA § 309] and 1365 [CWA § 505] of this title, with sections 1311 [CWA § 301], 1317

[CWA § 307], and 1343 [CWA § 403] of this title." 33 U.S.C. § 1344(p).

Here again, their argument is that silence is significant. Section 404(p) protects the permitee from lawsuits alleging violations of CWA § 301 (which bars the discharge of "any pollutant" "except as in compliance" with the Act), § 307 (which bars the discharge of "toxic pollutants"); and § 403 (which bars discharges into the sea). But § 404(p) does not in express terms protect the permitee from a lawsuit alleging a violation of § 306(e) or of the EPA's new source performance standards. Section 404(p)'s silence regarding § 306 is made even more significant because a parallel provision in § 402 does protect a § 402 permitee from an enforcement action alleging a violation of § 306. CWA § 402(k), 33 U.S.C. § 1342(k).

In our view, Congress' omission of § 306 from § 404, and its inclusion of § 306 in § 402(k), is evidence that Congress did not intend § 306(e) to apply to Corps § 404 permits or to discharges of fill material. If § 306 did apply, then the Corps would be required to evaluate each permit application for compliance with § 306, and issue a permit only if it found the discharge would comply with § 306. But even if that finding were made, it is not clear that the § 404 permitee would be protected from a suit seeking a judicial determination that the discharge violates § 306.

(3) The CWA is ambiguous on the question whether § 306 applies to discharges of fill material regulated under § 404. On the one hand, § 306 provides that a discharge that violates an EPA new source performance standard is "unlawful—without any exception for fill material. On the other hand, § 404 grants the Corps blanket authority to permit the discharge of fill material—without any mention of § 306. This tension indicates that Congress has not 'directly spoken' to the 'precise question' of whether § 306 applies to discharges of fill material." *Chevron* [casebook, pp. 1197–1200].

[III.B] Before turning to how the agencies have resolved that question, we consider the formal regulations that bear on §§ 306 and 404. See *Mead* [casebook, pp. 1213–23]. The regulations, like the statutes, do not address the question whether § 306, and the EPA new source performance standards promulgated under it, apply to § 404 permits and the discharges they authorize. There is no regulation, for example, interpreting § 306(e)'s text—"standard of performance applicable to such source"—to mean that a performance standard ceases to be "applicable" the moment the discharge qualifies as fill material, which would resolve the cases in petitioners' favor. Nor is there a regulation providing that the Corps, in deciding whether to grant a permit under § 404, must deny that permit if the discharge would violate § 306(e), which would decide the cases for SEACC.

Rather than address the tension between §§ 306 and 404, the regulations instead implement the statutory framework without elaboration on this point. Each of the two principal regulations, which have been mentioned above, seems to stand on its own without reference to the other. The EPA's new source performance standard contains no exception for fill material; and it forbids any discharge of "process wastewater," a term that includes solid wastes. 40 CFR § 440.104(b)(1). The agencies' joint regulation defining fill material is also unqualified. It includes "slurry, or tailings or similar mining-related materials" in its definition of a "discharge of fill material," 40 CFR § 232.2; and it contains no exception for slurry that is regulated by an EPA performance standard. * * *

[III.C.]   The regulations do not give a definitive answer to the question whether § 306 applies to discharges regulated by the Corps under § 404, but we do find that agency interpretation and agency application of the regulations are instructive and to the point. *Auer*. The question is addressed and resolved in a reasonable and coherent way by the practice and policy of the two agencies, all as recited in a memorandum written in May 2004 by Diane Regas, then the Director of the EPA's Office of Wetlands, Oceans and Watersheds, to Randy Smith, the Director of the EPA's regional Office of Water with responsibility over the mine. (Regas Memorandum). The Memorandum, though not subject to sufficiently formal procedures to merit *Chevron* deference, see *Mead*, is entitled to a measure of deference because it interprets the agencies' own regulatory scheme. See *Auer*.

The Regas Memorandum explains:

"As a result [of the fact that the discharge is regulated under § 404], the regulatory regime applicable to discharges under section 402, including effluent limitations guidelines and standards, such as those applicable to gold ore mining ... do not apply to the placement of tailings into the proposed impoundment [of Lower Slate Lake]. See 40 CFR § 122.3(b)."

The regulation that the Memorandum cites—40 CFR § 122.3—is one we considered above and found ambiguous. That regulation provides: "[d]ischarges of dredged or fill material into waters of the United States which are regulated under section 404 of CWA" "do not require [§ 402] permits." The Regas Memorandum takes an instructive interpretive step when it explains that because the discharge "do[es] not require" an EPA permit, the EPA's performance standard "do[es] not apply" to the discharge. The Memorandum presents a reasonable interpretation of the regulatory regime. We defer to the interpretation because it is not "plainly erroneous or inconsistent with the regulation[s]." *Auer*. Five factors inform that conclusion.

First, the Memorandum preserves a role for the EPA's performance standard. It confines the Memorandum's scope to closed bodies of water, like the lake here. When slurry is discharged into a closed body of water, the Memorandum explains, the EPA's performance standard retains an important role in regulating the discharge into surrounding waters. The Memorandum does not purport to invalidate the EPA's performance standard.

Second, the Memorandum acknowledges that this is not an instance in which the discharger attempts to evade the requirements of the EPA's performance standard. The Kensington Mine is not, for example, a project that smuggles a discharge of EPA-regulated pollutants into a separate discharge of Corps-regulated fill material. The instant cases do not present a process or plan designed to manipulate the outer boundaries of the definition of "fill material" by labeling minute quantities of EPA-regulated solids as fill. The Memorandum states that when a discharge has only an "incidental filling effect," the EPA's performance standard continues to govern that discharge.

Third, the Memorandum's interpretation preserves the Corps' authority to determine whether a discharge is in the public interest. See 33 CFR § 320.4(a)(1); 40 CFR § 230.10. The Corps has significant expertise in making this determination. Applying it, the Corps determined that placing slurry in the lake will improve that body of water by making it wider, shallower, and so more capable of sustaining aquatic life. The Corps determined, furthermore, that the alternative—a heap of tailings larger than the Pentagon placed upon wetlands—would cause more harm to the environment. Because the Memorandum preserves an important role for the Corps' expertise, its conclusion that the EPA's performance standard does not apply is a reasonable one.

Fourth, the Regas Memorandum's interpretation does not allow toxic pollutants (as distinguished from other, less dangerous pollutants, such as slurry) to enter the navigable waters. The EPA has regulated toxic pollutants under a separate provision, § 307 of the CWA, and the EPA's § 404(b) guidelines require the Corps to deny a § 404 permit for any discharge that would violate the EPA's § 307 toxic-effluent limitations. 40 CFR § 230.10(b)(2).

Fifth, as a final reason to defer to the Regas Memorandum, we find it a sensible and rational construction that reconciles §§ 306, 402, and 404, and the regulations implementing them, which the alternatives put forward by the parties do not. SEACC's argument, that § 402 applies to this discharge and not § 404, is not consistent with the statute and regulations, as already noted. See Part II, *supra.* * * *

[III.D   Justice Kennedy then proceeded to reject SEACC's argument that three agency statements—a 1986 "memorandum of understanding" between the EPA and the Corps regarding the definition of fill material, the preamble to the agencies' fill regulation (i.e., 40 CFR § 122.3), and remarks made by the agencies in response to public comments on the proposed fill regulation—contradicted the Regas Memorandum's interpretation of the memorandum.]

JUSTICE BREYER, concurring.

As I understand the Court's opinion, it recognizes a legal zone within which the regulating agencies might reasonably classify material either as "dredged or fill material" subject to § 404 of the Clean Water Act, 33 U.S.C. § 1344(a), or as a "pollutant," subject to §§ 402 and 306, 33 U.S.C.

§§ 1342(a), 1316(a). Within this zone, the law authorizes the environmental agencies to classify material as the one or the other, so long as they act within the bounds of relevant regulations, and provided that the classification, considered in terms of the purposes of the statutes and relevant regulations, is reasonable.

This approach reflects the difficulty of applying §§ 402 and 306 literally to *every* new-source-related discharge of a "pollutant." The Environmental Protection Agency (EPA) applies § 306 new source "performance standards" to a wide variety of discharges * * *. These "standards of performance" "reflect the greatest degree of effluent reduction which the Administrator determines to be achievable through application of the best available demonstrated control technology ... including, where practicable, a standard permitting no discharge of pollutants." 33 U.S.C. § 1316(a)(1). (1996).

To literally apply these performance standards so as to forbid the use of any of these substances as "fill," even when, say, they constitute no more than trace elements in dirt, crushed rock, or sand that is clearly being used as "fill" to build a levee or to replace dirt removed from a lake bottom may prove unnecessarily strict, cf. § 1362(6) (defining "pollutant" to include "rock"), to the point that such application would undermine the objective of § 404, which foresees the use of "dredged or fill material" in certain circumstances and with approval of the relevant agencies. § 1344. At minimum, the EPA might reasonably read the statute and the applicable regulations as allowing the use of such material, say crushed rock, as "fill" in some of these situations. Cf. *Chevron*; *Auer*.

At the same time, I recognize the danger that Justice Ginsburg warns against, namely, that "[w]hole categories of regulated industries" might "gain immunity from a variety of pollution-control standards," if, say, a § 404–permit applicant simply adds "sufficient solid matter" to a pollutant "to raise the bottom of a water body," thereby turning a "pollutant" governed by § 306 into "fill" governed by § 404. (1996).

Yet there are safeguards against that occurring. For one thing, as the Court recognizes, it is not the case that *any* material that has the "effect of ... [c]hanging the bottom elevation" of the body of water is automatically subject to § 404, not § 402. The EPA has never suggested that it would interpret the regulations so as to turn § 404 into a loophole, permitting evasion of a "performance standard" simply because a polluter discharges enough pollutant to raise the bottom elevation of the body of water. For another thing, even where a matter is determined reasonably to be "fill" and consequently falls within § 404, the EPA can retain an important role in the permitting process. That is because the EPA may veto any § 404 plan that it finds has an "unacceptable adverse effect on municipal water supplies, shellfish beds and fishery areas ..., wildlife, or recreational areas." § 1344(c). Finally, EPA's decision not to apply § 306, but to allow permitting to proceed under § 404, must be a reasonable decision; and court review will help assure that is so. 5 U.S.C. § 706.

In these cases, it seems to me that the EPA's interpretation of the statute as permitting the EPA/Corps of Engineers "fill" definition to apply to the cases at hand is reasonable, hence lawful. * * *

I cannot say whether the EPA's compromise represents the best overall environmental result; but I do believe it amounts to the kind of detailed decision that the statutes delegate authority to the EPA, not the courts, to make (subject to the bounds of reasonableness). I believe the Court's views are consistent with those I here express. And with that understanding, I join its opinion.

JUSTICE SCALIA, concurring in part and concurring in the judgment.

I join the opinion of the Court, except for its protestation that it is not according *Chevron* deference to the reasonable interpretation set forth in the [Regas Memorandum]—an interpretation consistently followed by both EPA and the Corps of Engineers, and adopted by both agencies in the proceedings before this Court. See *Chevron*. The opinion purports to give this agency interpretation "a measure of deference" because it involves an interpretation of "the agencies' own regulatory scheme," and "the regulatory regime" (citing *Auer*). *Auer*, however, stands only for the principle that we defer to an agency's interpretation *of its own ambiguous regulation*. But it becomes obvious from the ensuing discussion that the referenced "regulatory scheme" and "regulatory regime" for which the Court accepts the agency interpretation includes not just the agencies' own regulations but also (and indeed primarily) the conformity of those regulations with the ambiguous governing statute, which is the primary dispute here.

Surely the Court is not adding to our already inscrutable opinion in *Mead* the irrational fillip that an agency position which otherwise does not qualify for *Chevron* deference *does* receive *Chevron* deference if it clarifies not just an ambiguous statute but *also* an ambiguous regulation. One must conclude, then, that if today's opinion is *not* according the agencies' reasonable and authoritative interpretation of the Clean Water Act *Chevron* deference, it is according some *new* type of deference—perhaps to be called in the future *Coeur Alaska* deference—which is identical to *Chevron* deference except for the name.

The Court's deference to the EPA and the Corps of Engineers in today's cases is eminently reasonable. It is quite impossible to achieve predictable (and relatively litigation-free) administration of the vast body of complex laws committed to the charge of executive agencies without the assurance that reviewing courts will accept reasonable and authoritative agency interpretation of ambiguous provisions. If we must not call that practice *Chevron* deference, then we have to rechristen the rose. Of course the only reason a new name is required is our misguided opinion in *Mead*, whose incomprehensible criteria for *Chevron* deference have produced so much confusion in the lower courts that there has now appeared the phenomenon of *Chevron* avoidance—the practice of declining to opine whether *Chevron* applies or not.

I favor overruling *Mead*. Failing that, I am pleased to join an opinion that effectively ignores it.

JUSTICE GINSBURG, with whom JUSTICE STEVENS and JUSTICE SOUTER join, dissenting. * * *

The litigation before the Court * * * presents a single question: Is a pollutant discharge prohibited under § 306 of the Act eligible for a § 404 permit as a discharge of fill material? In agreement with the Court of Appeals, I would answer no. The statute's text, structure, and purpose all mandate adherence to EPA pollution-control requirements. A discharge covered by a performance standard must be authorized, if at all, by EPA.

[I.A] Congress enacted the Clean Water Act in 1972 "to restore and maintain the chemical, physical, and biological integrity" of the waters of the United States. 33 U.S.C. § 1251(a). "The use of any river, lake, stream or ocean as a waste treatment system," the Act's drafters stated, "is unacceptable." S.Rep. No. 92–414, p. 7 (1971). Congress announced in the Act itself an ambitious objective: to eliminate, by 1985, the discharge of all pollutants into the Nation's navigable waters. 33 U.S.C. § 1251(a). * * *

The Act instructs EPA to establish various technology-based, increasingly stringent effluent limitations for categories of point sources. *E.g.,* §§ 1311, 1314. * * *

Of key importance, new sources must meet stringent "standards of performance" adopted by EPA under § 306. That section makes it "unlawful for *any* . . . new source to operate . . . in violation of" an applicable performance standard. 33 U.S.C. § 1316(e) (emphasis added). * * *

In 1982, EPA promulgated new source performance standards for facilities engaged in mining, including those using a froth-flotation milling process. Existing mills, the Agency found, were already achieving zero discharge; it was therefore practicable, EPA concluded, for new mills to do as well. Accordingly, under 40 CFR § 440.104(b)(1), new mines using the froth-flotation method, as Coeur Alaska proposes to do, may not discharge wastewater directly into waters of the United States. * * *

[II] Is a pollutant discharge prohibited under § 306(e) eligible to receive a § 404 permit as a discharge of fill material? All agree on preliminary matters. Only one agency, the Corps or EPA, can issue a permit for the discharge. Only EPA, through the [§ 402 permitting scheme], issues permits that implement § 306. Further, § 306(e) and EPA's froth-flotation performance standard, unless inapplicable here, bar Coeur Alaska's proposed discharge. * * *

Section 404, stating that the Corps "may issue permits" for the discharge of "dredged or fill material," does not create an exception to § 306(e)'s plain command. 33 U.S.C. § 1344(a). Section 404 neither mentions § 306 nor states a contrary requirement. The Act can be home to both provisions, with no words added or omitted, so long as the category of "dredged or fill material" eligible for a § 404 permit is read in harmony with § 306. Doing so yields a simple rule: Discharges governed by EPA performance standards are subject to EPA's administration and receive permits under [§ 402], not § 404.

This reading accords with the Act's structure and objectives. It retains, through [§ 402], uniform application of the Act's core pollution-control requirements, and it respects Congress' special concern for new sources. Leaving pollution-related decisions to EPA, moreover, is consistent with Congress' delegation to that agency of primary responsibility to administer the Act. Most fundamental, adhering to § 306(e)'s instruction honors the overriding statutory goal of eliminating water pollution, and Congress' particular rejection of the use of navigable waters as waste disposal sites.

The Court's reading, in contrast, strains credulity. A discharge of a pollutant, otherwise prohibited by firm statutory command, becomes lawful if it contains sufficient solid matter to raise the bottom of a water body, transformed into a waste disposal facility. Whole categories of regulated industries can thereby gain immunity from a variety of pollution-control standards. * * *

Congress, we have recognized, does not "alter the fundamental details of a regulatory scheme in vague terms or ancillary provisions—it does not, one might say, hide elephants in mouseholes." *Whitman v. American Trucking Assns., Inc.,* 531 U.S. 457, 467–468 (2001). Yet an alteration of that kind is just what today's decision imagines. Congress, as the Court reads the Act, silently upended, in an ancillary permitting provision, its painstaking pollution-control scheme. Congress did so, the Court holds, notwithstanding the lawmakers' stated effort "to restore and maintain the chemical, physical, and biological integrity" of the waters of the United States, 33 U.S.C. § 1251(a); their assignment to EPA of the Herculean task of setting strict effluent limitations for many categories of industrial sources; and their insistence that new sources meet even more ambitious standards, not subject to exception or variance. Would a rational legislature order exacting pollution limits, yet call all bets off if the pollutant, discharged into a lake, will raise the water body's elevation? To say the least, I am persuaded, that is not how Congress intended the Clean Water Act to operate. * * *

NOTES ON COEUR ALASKA AND DEFERENCE TO AGENCY INTERPRETATIONS OF THEIR OWN RULES

1. *The Bootstrapping Concern with* Auer *Deference.* Justice Kennedy depicts the Regas Memorandum as an interpretation of the "regulatory scheme" and the "regulatory regime." Was the memorandum interpreting only the ambiguous EPA regulation, or was it construing the relevant provisions of the CWA as well?

If Justice Kennedy is treating the memorandum as an interpretation not only of the regulation, but also, by extension, of the statute, then he seems to be countenancing the kind of "bootstrapping" that concerned him in *Gonzales v. Oregon*.[a] Here, the EPA promulgated an ambiguous regulation to implement an ambiguous statute. It then interpreted the regulation in an internal memorandum. As an interpretation of the regulation, the memorandum should be assessed under *Auer* and should receive deference so long as that interpretation is not "plainly erroneous or inconsistent with the regulation" (casebook, pp. 1242–45). But insofar as the interpretation of the regulation also resolves an ambiguity in the statute, the memorandum should be assessed under *Chevron* and should receive deference only if its resolution of the statutory ambiguity is "reasonable" (casebook, pp. 1197–1200). To assess the agency's *statutory* interpretation under *Auer*, simply because it is embedded in an interpretation of a regulation, would be to permit the agency to bootstrap that interpretation from *Chevron* to the (possibly) more deferential *Auer* regime.

Justice Kennedy fails—at least explicitly—to assess the memorandum under the *Chevron* standard. Instead, he concludes his analysis by asserting that the memorandum satisfies the *Auer* standard. Insofar as the memorandum also interprets the statute, Justice Kennedy should have taken the further step of ensuring that, per *Chevron*, there had been a delegation of lawmaking authority and that the agency lawmaking was "reasonable." See *Mead* (casebook, pp. 1213–23).

This amounts to both substantive and procedural bootstrapping. It is *substantive*, as it enables an agency to shift its statutory interpretation from one regime of judicial review (*Chevron*) to a (possibly) more deferential one (*Auer*). It is *procedural,* as it enables the agency to reap the advantages of lawmaking without considering whether Congress has delegated that kind of authority (*Mead*). It does not appear that the Regas Memorandum was issued under a delegation of lawmaking authority, however. Thus, if the majority is tacitly treating the memorandum as a *statutory* interpretation, then it is allowing the agency to circumvent *Mead*. (Justice Kennedy elides this point— but Justice Scalia waves it like a bloody flag.)

Justice Ginsburg's dissenting opinion drives home the bootstrapping charge in another way: Under cover of *Auer*, the agency has radically amended the statutory scheme, creating a huge loophole for "fill" material to elbow out the strict no-tolerance EPA policy toward mining slurry. Her elephants-not-in-mouseholes argument is very similar to the one that Justice Kennedy found cogent in *Oregon*. (What *does* distinguish *Oregon* from *Coeur Alaska* for Justice Kennedy?)

2. *The Difference Between* Chevron *and* Auer? *And the Closeted Role of* Skidmore! Justice Scalia suggests that the majority is actually applying *Chevron* deference to the Regas Memorandum, despite its claim to be applying *Auer* deference. Is there any practical difference between the two regimes? That is, will judges be any more deferential under a "clearly erroneous" standard than under a "reasonableness" one? Or will they simply make an independent, policy-based judgment about the merits of deference in any

a. Indeed, in Part II.A., Justice Kennedy grants *Auer* deference to the EPA's interpretation of another regulation that "essentially restates the text of [the statute]"—the very kind of "parroting regulation" that Justice Kennedy refused to accord *Auer* deference in *Oregon*. What explains the different treatments?

given case, regardless of the particular deference regime they ultimately announce? This might be an implication of Justice Breyer's concurring opinion here, as well as his opinions in earlier cases. From Breyer's perspective, there is in reality just one deference regime: *Skidmore*, with its various factors for assessing whether deference is warranted (casebook, pp. 1194–95).

Bring these two points together and relate them to the majority opinion. Justice Kennedy claims to be according the Regas Memorandum "a measure of deference"—a phrase that appears to equivocate between *Chevron* and *Auer* deference. Note also that the five factors he adduces for deferring to the memorandum (especially the third, agency expertise) seem to sit comfortably within the *Skidmore* framework.

3.   *The Agency's Highly Dynamic Interpretation.* SEACC argued that the Regas interpretation was contradicted by three previous agency statements: a 1986 "memorandum of understanding" between the EPA and the Corps regarding the definition of fill material, which, though not subject to notice and comment procedures, was published in the Federal Register; the preamble of the current fill regulation; and remarks made by the agencies in response to public comments on the proposed fill regulation, remarks that were incorporated by reference into the administrative record.

Justice Kennedy concluded that the previous statements did not in fact contradict the Regas Memorandum, but there was strong evidence going the other way. G. Tracy Mehan, III, the former EPA Assistant Administrator for Water (2001–03) who oversaw the promulgation of the fill rule, filed an *amicus* brief supporting SEACC. Mehan advocated an interpretation of the rule that contradicted the one advanced in the Regas Memorandum, citing some of the very same agency statements noted above.[b] Does an agency enjoy *Auer* deference even after it has radically changed earlier constructions? Justice Kennedy did not answer that question, because he believed the EPA had been reasonably consistent in its approach to these issues.

The most dramatic agency volte-face, however, was the Corps' reinterpretation of "fill material." Given the Corps' longstanding jurisdiction over river-based construction and fill projects, the agency had apparently not, before the George W. Bush Administration, understood fill material to include elements that were mainly "pollutants" regulated primarily by EPA. Indeed, § 404 may cement the traditional definition of "fill material" into the statute. To begin with, § 404's use of the term "fill material" presumptively entails the materials the Corps had traditionally regulated, which were construction-related matter where the primary concern was that they would elevate water levels. Moreover, § 404(f)(1) exempts from Corps regulation fill materials resulting from construction or navigation activities (like constructing "farm roads," "dams," and the like). Finally, this reading of "fill material" contrasts with "pollutant," the matter regulated by the EPA. As a structural matter, this helps us understand why Congress treated §§ 402 and 404 as different

---

b.   Moreover, the Regas Memorandum may contradict the CWA itself. In addition to the arguments adduced by Justice Ginsburg's dissenting opinion, consider the relevance of CWA § 101(d): "Except as otherwise *expressly provided* ... the Administrator of the Environmental Protection Agency ... shall administer this [Act]." 33 U.S.C. § 1251(d) (emphasis added). Nothing in § 404 *explicitly* deprives the EPA of its primary jurisdiction over pollutants, and § 402 and the other anti-pollutant provisions seem to confirm the EPA's primary jurisdiction here.

regulatory regimes that presumptively did not overlap. (An *amicus* brief from members of Congress serving on committees regulating environmental matters made these points.)

Yet Justice Kennedy treated the Corps' definition of "fill material" (to include slurry) as settled between the parties and therefore not available for judicial second-guessing. Was this well founded? (*Amicus* briefs filed by both Tracy Meehan and the Members of Congress vigorously disputed this assertion and viewed it as central to the case.) Is the Bush Administration's expansion of the definition of fill material a regulatory elephant sneaking in through the statutory mousehole? Is the majority doing a disservice to the rule of law by going along with an administrative revision of the CWA—a revision that the *amici* felt were a wholesale abandonment of the statute's purpose, to clean up the nation's waterways?[c] How might Justice Breyer's concurring opinion help explain, or defend, the majority's approach?

4. Does Agency Deference Apply to Issues of Preemption?

Page 1268. Insert the following Case and Note after the Notes to *Geier*:

Wyeth v. Levine, 129 S.Ct. 1187 (2009). Directly injecting the drug Phenergan into a patient's vein creates a significant risk of catastrophic consequences. A Vermont jury found that Wyeth, the manufacturer of the drug, had failed to provide an adequate warning of that risk, and awarded damages to Diana Levine to compensate her for the amputation of her arm. Because the warnings on Phenergan's label had been deemed sufficient by the federal Food and Drug Administration (FDA) when it approved Wyeth's new drug application in 1955 and when it later approved changes in the drug's labeling, Wyeth challenged the state tort verdict on the ground that it was preempted by the Food, Drug & Cosmetic Act of 1938 (FDCA), which bars unsafe drugs.

Justice Stevens' opinion for the Court (joined by **Justices Kennedy, Souter, Ginsburg**, and **Breyer**) ruled that the FDCA did not preempt these state tort claims. Justice Stevens started with this presumption: "[i]n all pre-emption cases, and particularly in those in which Congress has 'legislated ... in a field which the States have traditionally occupied,' ... we 'start with the assumption that the historic police powers of the States were not to be superseded by the Federal Act unless that was the clear and manifest purpose of Congress.' " Quoting *Medtronic, Inc. v. Lohr*, 518 U.S. 470, 485 (1996).

---

c. See *Amicus* Brief of Tracy Meehan at 40–41: "Here, the proposed discharges would kill event fish in a pristine Alaskan Lake, and eliminate the natural processes and functions of an ecosystem for over a decade. It is difficult to fathom a result so diametrically opposed to the fundamental objective of the CWA. Respondents assert that they would restore the lake and restock fish in some ten to fifteen years, after mining operations cease. Even assuming that such restoration is possible, the restoration proposed here is inconsistent with Congressional intent that any environmental changes from discharges should be restored through natural processes, not dubious artificial restoration, and that natural processes should be restored within 'a few hours, days, or weeks,' not decades."

Wyeth's main argument rested upon a 2007 amendment to the FDCA that required FDA approval of drug labels. Because the FDA had okayed the warning that was the basis for the state tort suit, Wyeth argued that state tort law was implicitly preempted because it would be impossible for Wyeth to comply with both its federal duty to use the approved label and its state duty to provide more detailed warnings (the doctrine of "impossibility preemption"). In an *amicus* brief, the FDA agreed and urged the Court to find preemption here. Justice Stevens rejected that argument, in part because federal law allowed Wyeth to amend its label without FDA approval based on safety concerns of the sort raised by the state tort suit. Thus, it was *not* impossible for Wyeth to comply with both federal law and state law. More generally, Justice Stevens ruled that the federal statute vests primary responsibility for labeling with drug companies, not the FDA, which is merely a monitor.

Wyeth and the FDA also argued that state tort liability undermined the purposes of federal law (the doctrine of "obstacle preemption"). In a preface to a 2006 rule, the FDA had opined that drug standards in the statute represented *both* a floor *and* a ceiling for manufacturers; hence, state tort liability was preempted when the manufacturer was following the label requirements of the federal law.

"In prior cases, we have given 'some weight' to an agency's views about the impact of tort law on federal objectives when 'the subject matter is technica[l] and the relevant history and background are complex and extensive.' *Geier* [casebook, pp. 1262–66]. Even in such cases, however, we have not deferred to an agency's *conclusion* that state law is pre-empted. Rather, we have attended to an agency's explanation of how state law affects the regulatory scheme. While agencies have no special authority to pronounce on pre-emption absent delegation by Congress, they do have a unique understanding of the statutes they administer and an attendant ability to make informed determinations about how state requirements may pose an 'obstacle to the accomplishment and execution of the full purposes and objectives of Congress.' [See *Geier.*] The weight we accord the agency's explanation of state law's impact on the federal scheme depends on its thoroughness, consistency, and persuasiveness. Cf. *Mead* [casebook, pp. 1213–23]; *Skidmore* [casebook, pp. 1194–95].

"Under this standard, the FDA's 2006 preamble does not merit deference. When the FDA issued its notice of proposed rulemaking in December 2000, it explained that the rule would 'not contain policies that have federalism implications or that preempt State law.' In 2006, the agency finalized the rule and, without offering States or other interested parties notice or opportunity for comment, articulated a sweeping position on the FDCA's pre-emptive effect in the regulatory preamble. The agency's views on state law are inherently suspect in light of this procedural failure.

"Further, the preamble is at odds with what evidence we have of Congress' purposes, and it reverses the FDA's own longstanding position without providing a reasoned explanation, including any discussion of how state law has interfered with the FDA's regulation of drug labeling during decades of coexistence. The FDA's 2006 position plainly does not reflect the agency's own view at all times relevant to this litigation. Not once prior to Levine's injury did the FDA suggest that state tort law stood as an obstacle to its statutory mission. To the contrary, it cast federal labeling standards as a floor upon which States could build and repeatedly disclaimed any attempt to pre-empt failure-to-warn claims. For instance, in 1998, the FDA stated that it did 'not believe that the evolution of state tort law [would] cause the development of standards that would be at odds with the agency's regulations.' It further noted that, in establishing 'minimal standards' for drug labels, it did not intend 'to preclude the states from imposing additional labeling requirements.' "

Justice Breyer (the author of *Geier*) wrote a concurring opinion, reserving judgment on the possibility that the FDA could in the future adopt a rule having preemptive force (as in *Geier*) if the agency found a specific clash between federal policy and state tort lawsuits.

Justice Thomas concurred in the judgment. "I have become increasingly skeptical of this Court's 'purposes and objectives' pre-emption jurisprudence. Under this approach, the Court routinely invalidates state laws based on perceived conflicts with broad federal policy objectives, legislative history, or generalized notions of congressional purposes that are not embodied within the text of federal law." Drawing from the Tenth Amendment, the Constitution's federal structure, and Article I, § 7, Justice Thomas argued that, as a matter of constitutional principle, state law remains the default law for citizens unless there is a *federal statutory text* that preempts it under Article VI (the Supremacy Clause). Hence, he was skeptical of obstacle preemption doctrine entirely and would apply impossibility preemption doctrine very cautiously—and was unwilling to apply either doctrine to the Levine case.

Justice Alito (joined by **Chief Justice Roberts** and **Justice Scalia**) dissented. Justice Alito relied on the notion that the FDA is responsible for determining drug safety and, hence, that its determinations are both a floor and a ceiling for a manufacturer's legal responsibility. Cf. *Riegel v. Medtronic, Inc.,* 552 U.S. 312 (2008) (ruling that federal regulation preempts state tort suits for warning defects for medical devices, also regulated by the FDA).[d] Indeed, Justice Alito believed the case was controlled by *Geier.*

"Notwithstanding the statute's saving clause, and notwithstanding the fact that Congress gave the Secretary authority to set only 'minimum' safety standards, we held Geier's state tort suit pre-empted. In reaching that result, we relied heavily on the view of the Secretary of Transportation—expressed in an *amicus* brief—that Standard 208 'embodies the

---

d. The Court distinguished *Riegel* in part because the Medical Devices Act of 1976 included a preemption clause—in contrast to the Food, Drug & Cosmetics Act of 1938, which even as amended has never contained a preemption clause.

Secretary's policy judgment that safety would best be promoted if manufacturers installed *alternative* protection systems in their fleets rather than one particular system in every car.' Because the Secretary determined that a menu of alternative technologies was 'safe,' the doctrine of conflict pre-emption barred Geier's efforts to deem some of those federally approved alternatives 'unsafe' under state tort law.

"The same rationale applies here. Through Phenergan's label, the FDA offered medical professionals a menu of federally approved, 'safe' and 'effective' alternatives—including IV push—for administering the drug. Through a state tort suit, respondent attempted to deem IV push 'unsafe' and 'ineffective.' To be sure, federal law does not prohibit Wyeth from contraindicating IV push, just as federal law did not prohibit Honda from installing airbags in all its cars. But just as we held that States may not compel the latter, so, too, are States precluded from compelling the former. If anything, a finding of pre-emption is even more appropriate here because the FDCA—unlike the National Traffic and Motor Safety Vehicle Act—contains no evidence that Congress intended the FDA to set only 'minimum standards,' and the FDCA does not contain a saving clause."

NOTE ON WYETH AND AGENCY VIEWS IN PREEMPTION CASES

Professor Nina Mendelson argued in Chevron *and Preemption*, 102 Mich. L. Rev. 737 (2004), that *Chevron* deference should presumptively not be available for agency interpretations preempting state law (see the casebook's Note 3 to *Geier*, pp. 1267–68). *Wyeth* seems consistent with her position and reasoning. Consider other patterns we have discerned in the Supreme Court preemption decisions between 1984 and 2006:

- The Court was more skeptical of agency interpretations that expanded national power than of those that respected the regulatory authority of the states. When an agency argued against preemption (39 cases, 1984– 2006) the Court agreed with its assessment 84.6% of the time, an astounding rate of agreement. So *Wyeth* was squarely in the mainstream of Supreme Court practice in this regard.

- For technical areas of law, as in *Geier,* the Court was super-deferential: For the 31 cases involving transportation, energy, and communications, the Court agreed with agency recommendations (usually favoring preemption) a whopping 87.1% of the time. Health law cases, such as *Wyeth* and *Riegel,* had lower but still impressive agreement rates. Normative areas such as civil rights and criminal law saw much less impressive agency performances.

- There was no significant difference between agency win rates for express preemption cases (97 cases, with 72.2% agreement rate) and for conflict or obstacle preemption cases (29 cases, with 72.4% agreement rate), perhaps surprising in light of the Article I, § 7 and the federalism concerns raised by Justice Thomas against conflict or obstacle preemption in *Wyeth* and other cases.

See William N. Eskridge Jr., *Vetogates,* Chevron, *Preemption*, 83 Notre Dame L. Rev. 1441 (2008) (reporting and analyzing these data).

Note that federalism-loving Justice Scalia dissented in *Wyeth* and is probably unsympathetic to the Mendelson position. Why would a strong federalist favor an agency-driven preemption of traditional state law? Justice Thomas' position, also from a strong federalist orientation, is very different from Justice Scalia's. Accord, Bradford R. Clark, *Separation of Powers as a Safeguard of Federalism*, 79 Tex. L. Rev. 1321 (2001). Is there any principled reason a federalist should follow Justice Scalia over Justice Thomas as to this issue?

†